MIGRANT DESTINY

WRITER AND POET
MARLA RODAS

Jóvenes Escritores Latinos
info@editorialjel.org

*#JEL - Creando Activistas
a Través de las Letras*

MIGRANT DESTINY

Published by
Editorial #JEL Jóvenes Escritores Latinos
info@editorialjel.org
info@mbc-education.com
Printed in the United States of America

All rights reserved, 2021
Marla Rodas
escritoraypoetisamarlarodas@gmail.com

ISBN: 978-1-953207-30-2

Cover design by Frank Lugo
English translation by Jose Byron Gonzalez

Sales and distribution rights
Escritora Marla Rodas
All rights reserved. Except as permitted under U.S. Copyright Act of 1976, no part of this publication may be reproduced, distributed, or transmitted in any form or by any means, or stored in a database or retrieval system, without the prior written permission of the publisher.

MARLA RODAS DE RAMIREZ

From writer and poet Marla Rodas:

Millions of people migrate from their countries in search of opportunities and arrive in the United States to enrich this great nation. This phenomenon is known as a "brain drain" for the countries left behind and many times without ever again seeing their migrant citizens.

The case of Marla Rodas, born in Malacatán, San Marcos, Guatemala, is different. She left her beloved Guatemala when she was 18 years old and like a true ambassador of her culture, enriched the United States with her literary contributions, her great love for humankind, her sense of justice and she returned to her country of origin bringing the fruits of her work in order to help Guatemalan children.

That same desire to help children made her start Guate Escribe, a non-profit organization that offers academic support to many children so that they continue and complete their schooling and, like her, can work hard to become the pride of Guatemala.

Marla Rodas, a teacher by training, grew up under the loving care of her grandparents and became a mother to her two great loves: Abel and Julian. Marla is self-taught and a lover of knowledge; among her many studies, she completed coursework in Business Computing and Cosmetology, both in Miami, Florida.

She offers us an example of hard work and passionate support to positive causes such as gender equality and women's issues.

Writing is her greatest passion and she has written poetry for as long as she can remember. It was not until 2009 that she became formally involved in writing upon her participation in poetry contests at the Center for Poetry Studies (C.E.P.) in Madrid, Spain, where one of her poems "Terco Corazón" (Stubborn Heart) appears in the book "Palabras al Viento" (Words to the Wind) realizing another dream: to see her work published.

She has also taken part in short story competitions at Indeleble Editores in Guatemala.

Her work in letters is internationally recognized and her books have gained renown as part of the hispanic literary legacy.

In 2010 she published her first book **"Segmentos de Agonia" (Segments of Agony)** in the United States, which is available at Barnes & Noble as well as Amazon.com.

Her second book **"Caminos sin Rumbo" (Roads Without a Course)** was published in her beloved Guatemala in 2015.

Her third book **"Suspiros en Poesía" (Sighs in Poetry)** was published in the United States in 2017. Her fourth book **"Voces de la Humanidad" (Voices of Humanity)** is also published in the United States in 2019 and is currently available at Amazon.com

It should be noted that many of her literary contributions are listed under many different organizations and anthologies.

She realizes another dream as a writer with her first novel: **DESTINO MIGRANTE (MIGRANT DESTINY).**

In November 2017 Marla was named a Goodwill Ambassador for Golden Rules by Ambassador Clydes Rivers.

She was a member of the Ontario Hispanic Chamber of Commerce, www.onthcc.com.

She produced and hosted her show "Tu Voz es mi Voz" (Your Voice is my Voice) on Radio Centroamerica, www.radiocentroamerica.com, TuvozEsMiVoz502@gmail.com.

She was also a member of ADELA (Asociación de Escritores Latinoamericanos, Association of Latin American Writers).

Marla is currently director of the literary organization Jóvenes Escritores Latinos – Guatemala

(#JEL-Guatemala), through which young people and adults are motivated to become activists through literature; together with its youth team, she coordinated the youth-oriented anthology **"Cómo Salvar Nuestro Planeta ¡HOY!" (How to Save Our Planet... TODAY!)** which aims to awaken respect for the natural resources and health of the planet, at an early age.

This fabulous humanitarian and literary trajectory make Marla Rodas a true Guatemalan pride.

Miriam Burbano, Founder and President of **#JEL**
Los Angeles, California. 2020.

Dedications...

MIGRANT DESTINY is dedicated to brave men, who discovered my fears and locked me in the room to overcome them through my keyboard.

MIGRANT DESTINY is dedicated to Abel and Julián, who will forever be connected to me by blood and an umbilical cord that will never be severed, for it is forever connected to my heart and they are my motivation for wanting to achieve great things.

MIGRANT DESTINY is dedicated in memoriam to all the immigrants who passed away due to the Covid-19 pandemic.

Acknowledgement:

Forever grateful to my God for His infinite love and mercy towards myself.

I thank my grandparents who look down on me from Heaven. Thank you for having allowed me to dream in your magical stories..

Hely, Thank you!

Description:

MIGRANT DESTINY is a novel of many colors, of black and white and gray landscapes that appear from its beginning.

The seven generations that exist in this work endure a constant fight with destiny and people who want to take advantage in any way and at any cost, of our protagonists. The magnitude of the tragedies, the abyss that separates and the highs and lows experienced by each generation, making it ever more vulnerable but at the same time wiser and better at defending its honor.

Guatemala and the scene of so many tragedies that have seared the heart of its people is the same one that embraces these generations, whose realism is felt to such a degree that one does not know whether it is fiction or the same stage in which Guatemalans have lived. With its travels and wars, legends and joys, it touches the core of each generation, rises and descends to the bottom again. It is in each new beginning the happiness of an unhappy ending where truth repeats itself like a never ending fire.

With her imagination the author takes us on a trip, which once started, we don't want to end; reality and fiction are lines that weave themselves to give life to each generation and little by little takes us into that side of Guatemala that very few know: the witches and shamans with their dark angels, its demons with a full name; the hard-working people always looking for a better future, the mantles, red in blood and death that hide in the jungles, the trees with their truths hidden in the branches, the virtue of making the best of a bad situation, the bitterness of not giving up and selling out.

To read "MIGRANTE DESTINY" is to go into a reality that the world does not easily see, it is much more than a simple novel of fiction.

To understand it we must see life from an isolated vantage point for not all written in it is fiction; there will be those who cry the dead as their own and are filled with rage and sadness with the tragedies that take place here.

Marla Rodas aims to portray in this novel the life of many people who have grown up in Guatemala and lived with these colors, with the same scenes, humble people who in search of peace offer their trust to someone who does not deserve it, people whose hopes hang by a thread and believe the lies of those who only want to use them.

The grace and magic of this novel is endless, whoever is fortunate enough to read it will have the opportunity to understand, among many other things, those love stories without a happy ending and that, despite everything, those that with their truth and head held high go and try to change the world for the better, even if they lose their life in the attempt, will always be victorious.

"MIGRANT DESTINY" is, without a doubt, a fantastic novel, full of adventure, drama and suspense, very worthy of being read

Ismar Escobar
Poet and writer

MIGRANT DESTINY

FIRST GENERATION

Icy wind blasts caress the silky cheeks of the cherry tree flowers, welcoming the longed for month of April. Very similar to the absent disaffection in the life of that little boy, who sees from the window how the wind drags out the life of that flower; alone, lost, apart from the family core grows Roderick Meyer, Jr. So innocent and bold at his young age. He is educated with severity at the public school of his town; he doesn't seem to be intimidated by the huge boys that wanted to scare him with their taunts. Sitting like the other children with the only difference that his attention is truly focused on learning, as the smallest boy to complete elementary school and with the best grade.

He has only seen his father very few times, duty to his country keeps military man Roderick Meyer far from his family; he barely recognizes his face, present in his mind only due to the portrait that hangs in the cold and desolate living room next to old family photographs but, of course, including his parents' wedding.

The beautiful Katherine Klein evidences fatigue in her eyes, the shine of the blue that her eyes radiated has been lost. Since her husband joined the ranks of the army, she has lived alone in her own world, she only finds relief and solace writing love poems and every now and then, one of heartbreak, consequence of her beloved husband's absence. She can barely make out the message she writes, the water that springs from her eyes erases some of the letters. Since they married she has been locked in her room, waiting for the war's end and the return of her beloved husband, to finally make come true the life he promised her before an altar of cherry tree flowers. The years take their toll, consume her isolated among those four walls and she completely forgets that there is a little boy who needs his mother's care. He is the favorite of the housekeeper, the only one who gives him all her attention just not to see him so dejected; she has become his playmate. For what is worth, he is happy with [1]Oma, as he calls her.

She prepares his favorite dishes, even as Junior has asked to write down her recipes, so that when he marries his wife can make them exactly the same. In those few happy moments for Junior,

---

[1] Oma: Granny

his laughter resonates in that huge kitchen, echoing through all corners of the big house. His favorite moments are spent in the kitchen, eating his favorite preserve, cheese curds with pretzels and potatoes with sausage. He just loves his Oma's cooking. Afterwards, alone in his room, he sits by the window and enjoys the landscape as he studies, to try and ignore this loneliness; to not feel the same monotony, changes the scene to the living room, an identical view with the only difference that he can see who might be at the entrance to the house.

A year before completing secondary education he follows the same routine: sat in the same place, next to the same window of the living room, Junior Meyer sees a man that, for a moment, makes him believe it might be his father. Immediately darts to the door; the military man closest to Roderick Meyer brings to the door a parchment with the bad news. His eyes tear up upon reading the document; the soldier cannot help himself and grabs him in an embrace, trying to offer support or consolation, babbling some words tells him:

—[2]Es tut mir leid, mein herzliches beileid!

Junior glances at the photograph of the handsome soldier who lost his life in combat... at

---

[2] Es tut mir leid, mein herzliches beileid: I am sorry! My sincere condolences.

thirty four years of age.

Worry overwhelms him; how is he going to tell his mother his father is gone forever?, knowing the pain she has endured over his absence and fulfilling his patriotic duty. She, every morning of every day, sitting in her rocking chair, searching the horizon, always spends the early hours of the day awaiting the return of her beloved husband.

That was a very different day, very early in the morning she has requested a strong linden blossom tea, whose effect was not delayed and writing the verses of hope and longing for the embrace of her husband, the one she has loved from the day they met, she has fallen asleep.

Junior opens the door to his mother's room, careful not to make any sounds. He sees his mother slumped over the rough desk, the steel-pointed quill in her hand and her face covering the papers, full of poems (she had hundreds of them). He is frozen for a few seconds, scared, thinking the worst has happened, his mother is also dead. She feels his presence and straightens up right away. Quickly grabs the quill she dropped when startled and sighs in relief:

—Ah!, [3]Mein sohn du bist es!

Rising quickly, extending her arms, putting on a melancholic expression, with her teary eyes,

---

[3] **Mein sohn du bist es:** My son it's you

as if asking forgiveness for the absence. Her heart beats faster and faster, as her son gets close to her, she knows something bad has happened. Junior's hand trembles with the parchment and the foreboding makes her collapse. He runs to lift her but his strength abandons him in witnessing his mother's pain, without even having said a word. He says nothing and the embrace like never before; they cry together in each other's arms until they tire, without letting go. Laying on the cold floor, time passes without notice until the next morning.

The housekeeper enters without notice, as the door is still open. Frightened, she runs to them and moves them with frantic gestures, thinking death has taken both of them. They wake up, stunned at the rapid rise. Their eyes are sad, swollen and reddened; the housekeeper helps them rise without understanding what is happening, since she just returned after a few days away visiting her own family.

Preparations for the burial are complete, the beautiful Katharine can hardly stand on her own, her face evidences the agony within. Her son holds her by the arm to receive the expressions of condolence; the funeral had full military honors and, she notices, just as in their wedding day... The place is full of cherry flowers, the season coincides... again!

A year has slowly gone by since the funeral. Katherine has not yet recovered from that loss, his absence is overwhelming, she has not written any more poetry

Roderick Jr. prepares for a trip to another country, plans for him to continue his schooling outside Germany had been made before his father died. He is excited to see other places, has always dreamed of traveling all over the world although leaving his mother so sad, has made him desist. His mother sees him put away the belongings that some time ago were prepared for this trip, he explains his razon for suspending it.

Katherine knows that this trip has been a dream of his and had already been approved by his father. She convinces him by telling him:

—⁴Keine sorge, mir geht's gut, umso mehr, als ich weiß, dass mein sohn niemals aufgeben würde, seine träume zu verwirklichen.

Despite her emotional attrition this year they have shared so many unforgettable moments, they are closer than they have ever been, she could share quality time with her child. True, a disgrace had to happen for her to open her eyes and her

---

⁴Keine sorge, mir geht's gut, umso mehr, als ich weiß, dass mein sohn niemals aufgeben würde, seine träume zu verwirklichen: Don't worry, I'm fine, all the more as I know that my son would never give up on making his dreams come true.

heart to be able to enjoy her son's company. She is so saddened by Roderick Jr.'s trip but puts on her best face, drawing from her last reserves of strength, smiling at his happiness, while he fails to see she is dying inside.

Not one tear is shed when they say goodbye. She shows happiness so that he is at peace, without him knowing these are the last smiles he shall see on his mother's face and the last time her soft hands make the sign of the cross giving her final blessing. The last embrace!

Not a year has passed since he left when he receives the distressing news that his mother is bedridden. Sadness has consumed her in the blackest depressions and no one can make her leave that massive bed. He sets off at once, hoping to still find her alive and never again leave her side.

She has not written since her husband's death; she asks the housekeeper for paper and ink, with what little strength she has left she holds the quill and writes a last letter to her son. In it, she begs his forgiveness for the years of maternal absence, obsessed over the love to her husband; she also begs him not to be sad over her death, she will finally rest next to his father. She has already expressed her last wishes in her will, made of big parchments with a seal of legitimacy. She doesn't want her son to hold on to a place, for inheritance or nostalgy; she authorizes him to sell it all if he so desires. Junior does not arrive time on time and in her last sigh, she finishes her letter with: [5]*Ich liebe dich sohn!*

Roderick cries before his mother's body and follows her will. She is buried next to his father in the family cemetery as the season coincides yet again, cherry trees blooming and the graves looked like quilted carpets, just embroidered with supreme delicacy.

After burying his mother Roderick Jr. retakes his civil engineering career and remains in that bohemian town until graduation. Every now and then in his sober thoughts he admits surprise at his strength to overcome the loss of his parents; his devotion to his books helps lighten the pain of his loneliness.

He returns home after graduation, he doesn't want to stay for too long in a place that torments him with so many memories, both good and bad. His stay has been like dusk breaking into dawn, overnight. Just the absolute minimum to sell off his inheritance. He packs some belongings, among them his father's portrait, his parents' wedding, their wedding rings and a gold medallion that his mother wore through their marriage, a present from his father. He saves all the poems his mother wrote, among which he finds the recipes of

---

[5] Ich liebe dich sohn: I love you son

his favorite dishes by the housekeeper, his Oma who is helping him pack. He looks at the recipes and at Oma. With eyes full of tears, he embraces her.

She tells him that one day she asked his mother to write down the recipes, Junior Meyer tells her that he is taking those things most valuable to him, especially her recipes. The rest are simple possessions without meaning.

For the love and faithful work the housekeeper did for his family, he gifts her the big house. Crying disconsolately tells him whenever he wishes to return, it is and will always be his house. In an endless embrace he bids her goodbye, swearing he will stay in touch with her, regardless where in the world he might be.

Before leaving he visits his parents' grave, bringing the cherry flowers his mother loved so much; the entire surroundings of the house are full of them. The season coincides… yet again!

His sighs merge with salty tears, some of which shower the flower buds, still in his hands. The knot in his throat overcomes him and he sobs his farewell words:

—[6]Auf wiedersehen liebe eltern, auf wiedersehen Sajonia!

---

[6] Auf wiedersehen liebe eltern, auf wiedersehen Sajonia: Goodbye dear parents, goodbye Sajonia.

He changes the course of his life, regardless of the risks or challenges he must face. Travel takes a very long time from one country to another, however that has not stopped Junior Meyer; he loves adventure and the unknown. His travels take him to France, his fascination for different cultures and the arts lead him to take on two careers simultaneously, Archaeology and Anthropology.

He remains there only the time required to complete his studies.

Again he packs his belongings with sentimental value and sets on the road to Barcelona, where some of his classmates who have already been to Spain excite his thoughts with tales of that magical place. He has been self-taught since he remembers and languages have never been a problem for him, nothing prevents him from starting a new adventure.

He registers in a literature course; the mysteries of history fill him with desire to be always in the library, hungry for knowledge reading book after book.

In his class he meets two young men from Guatemala City, of Spanish ascent. They could remain in Spain if they were so inclined; one of them is staying with his grandparents right there in Barcelona. Despite the quick academic advancements in their country of origin, these young men's parents insisted they graduate from a university in their own country of origin. They do everything to please their parents, from speaking in perfect Castilian to finding themselves in a place which, it could be argued, is the "mother country" to their own, they still don't fit. They experience some discrimination as they are considered criollos and while that is not a concern for them, since they love their native country, they find the casual cruelty of some humans very unsettling.

In a very short time they bond in friendship with Junior Meyer, so much so that Antonio asks his grandparents to let his friend stay with them through the end of the school year

They speak so much and so fondly of their country, of nature, its archaeology, Mayan culture, perfect weather, its beautiful women and such wonders that Junior's curiosity is piqued; they offer him a place to stay should he ever travel to lovely Guatemala.

It was during the last days of school when the days felt endless to them. In a few more, they will be back in their country. Antonio's grandparents hope that he'd never leave again but his decision to return stands. It's farewell day and everyone is about to leave when they see Junior Meyer with his bags packed.

Francisco and Antonio exchange glances,

Antonio tells Junior that he doesn't need to leave right away, it is them who must return home. He can stay as long as he wants, so long as the grandparents agree and they both burst out laughing. Junior Meyer jokingly tells them it won't be so easy to get rid of him, he has decided to travel with them and visit that wondrous country they have described for him.

Junior Meyer, graduate from the best schools in different countries and with the best grades, is consequently a fluent speaker in many languages and a collection of degrees.

The long trip makes Junior delirious about that place; sometimes he falls in such a deep sleep he thinks he can hear the sirens' song, waking up in a sweat. His anxiety gives him away, he reads and asks his friends all he can about their country. After many days and nights they arrive to the Gulf of Mexico coasts, where Junior believes the journey is finished however his friend Antonio, in a peculiar Spanish accent, full of "z"s, disillusions him of that notion by telling him:

—We're not there yet, my friend, we still have a few days of horse riding to reach the Pacific coast, where we'll take another boat to get to Guatemala, then we'll be close to home.

In a rush, he seeks out the coaches heading for their Pacific port of call.

They're making good time and are very

lucky to find one departing that same day, otherwise the long days of wait would have been ones of despair in the suffocating heat; it's smell so strong, Francisco's stomach can bear it no more. Despite a few inconveniences, something magical follows them and helps them along, the universe itself glows for them.

From faraway lands Junior Meyer stands upon Guatemalan soil. A strange energy runs through his body when his feet touch it, making a lifelong connection. His skin color and even his name is not overlooked, attracting the attention of the shy young ladies of the local society. Some in a rush to travel, leave a smile for the handsome Junior Meyer, others, walk to the rhythm of their uncomfortable shoes while yet others hope to find love brought by the large vessels.

With only twenty-nine years of age, full of life, our handsome intellectual adventurer finds himself on the Guatemalan Pacific coast. His pale cheeks turn the shade of two red apples; the heat is stifling yet he cannot remove his formal suit. Looking all around he hopes for a place to save him from this sun clouding his senses. The dark blue of his eyes is lost in the depths of the ocean, without finding a safe harbor.

Unable to resist it anymore, he cries:

—⁷Heiliger Gott, wie heiß!

His friends draw close to him laughing out loud and Antonio, with his peculiar Spanish accent tells him:

—Well, well! You're melting, this coastal area is hot and humid but things will get better in the city, you'll see, it's always spring there.

Poor Junior Meyer, almost unable to breath and with a accent that made "r" sound like "j" says:

—Well, well! Then we must find a way to get to the city before I die of heatstroke. ¡I don't want to die so young!

His friends are still laughing since he really looks about to pass out. It's a perfect time to continue on their way to Guatemala de la Asunción.

Now much closer to their destination, Meyer seems hypnotized by the beauty he admires, every place his eyes can reach is different yet still beautiful. Everyone sleeps while he writes down his experiences and the contrasting beauty of this mystical place.

Everything he has seen up to now seems fascinating; not even in his best dreams or the most advanced cities can be compared to such ineffable beauty. Through every place he goes

---

⁷ Heiliger Gott, wie heiß: Holy god how hot.

through he falls madly in love with this land. He never wants to go!

It certainly is not a very advanced country, not like the other places he's been. The magic of its natural beauty overwhelms him. He's reached a place which he never imagined thanks to his friends' insistence. Finally they reach Guatemala de la Asunción, the capital city; Francisco Rodriguez heads toward his ranch same as Antonio who is joined by his german friend.

The happiness of Antonio de la Vega's parents is boundless, they already prepared a party to welcome him after a four year absence. They are surprised at the handsome young man accompanying their son and he is promptly introduced as his best friend. They quickly set up a room which is way better than he expected.

So much has happened in his life that he sighs an expression of joy, standing before his door. Crossing it he places his heavy and worn luggage on the floor. Closes the door and leans against it. His lovely eyes look around, scanning each corner of the large room. The floor is wooden, which creaks with each step; near the window, an enormous dresser in a dark mahogany shade matched by an elegant wardrobe and a huge bed inviting him in for a nice nap, with matching night tables side by side, an oil lamp and a crystal jar with seasonal flowers, gardenias in this case.

At the end of the room a tasteful desk, where he places his leather bag and takes out his parents' photograph, holding it close to his chest, sighing and shedding a few tears.

He's so tired he drops into bed and wasn't heard from until the next day. He is awakened when they knock on his door, rising suddenly and startled, not knowing where to go and not sure of where he was; for a few minutes he is quiet and lies in silence until he hears

—Erick!, Erick!, this is Antonio.

Which is what he calls him since they met, "Erick" claiming it's easier and sounds more Spanish.

Junior Meyer nears the door, stubbing his toe with the luggage he left there last night, as tired as he was. Opens the door and sees his playful friend telling him:

—How did you rest? Breakfast awaits!

Junior Meyer only shakes his head not knowing how early or late it may be. Half asleep he answers:

—I'm going, I'm going…!

And without facing his friends softly closes the door. He heads for the dresses where he uses a porcelain pail, with its corresponding jar to wash his face and hands, heading towards the dining room at a fast pace. Greets his hosts and stands at attention.

Antonio tells him:

—You slept like a log!

And with his peculiar accent replies:

—I don't snore!

They all laugh and Antonio rises to meet him and with a few pats on the back tells him:

—Come, my good friend Erick, this is your place, right next to me!

Erick, still a little bewildered by all these events, offers excuses for not staying longer and later the night before in order to get to know them better. Antonio's mother tells him she understands how tired they were and how unwise of them it was to throw a party they knew they couldn't enjoy. Still happy with Antonio's return, the De la Vegas have planned another little shindig, with the cream of the local society, those closest to them.

Maria Antonieta de la Vega tells them before leaving for the kitchen:

—You have all morning to unpack and you can even nap, but I want you both ready and handsome by four in the evening.

Junior Meyer was well liked by Antonio's parents, they feel like they have known him his whole life, he's been fully accepted and they quickly take him in, almost like if he was another son.

After breakfast; Antonio takes Junior Meyer for a ride around their lands. He's been riding since he was a child, he's an able rider and is on his favorite horse, a hot-blooded black stallion. Roderick, instead, has been looking at books but is not entirely lacking riding abilities and quickly mounts the one offered by his friend.

Antonio tells him how they got their lands; few Spaniards have acres of lands, among them his parents, inherited from their grandparents, who due to a serious crisis in Spain invested their fortune in those lands.

Junior Meyer wants to win some property in that unique place. He can buy whatever he wants, money is no object, he carries with him his fortune in gold ingots.

—Let's go back home, Mom warned us to be on time for her darn party.

Antonio tells him, riding and laughing out loud, he challenges Junior Meyer. He, instead, pays him no mind, enjoys the landscape and gets closer to the ranch in a happy trot.

As dusk nears, the butler is standing erect and elegant by the door, awaiting the arrival of their guests. The sounds of the coaches arriving early, to the beat of the horses marching, led by the coachmen of each invited family. They all arrive with their best clothes, the bourgeoisie of the surrounding province, and very close friends to the De la Vega family, arriving little by little at the celebratory hall. Piano music plays for the lovers of classical music, tables are elegantly set and served, but they are still missing a few guests. A gorgeous young woman arrives, to the appreciative voice of the butler:

—Welcome, Marquise!

as she nods in thanks, with both elegance and humility. Her beauty radiates with each step, Antonio's mother receives her with delight. Clueless Francisco, flirty Antonio and Junior Meyer are talking, in a circle; when Meyer's eyes lose themselves in the Marquise's own, she looks away and continues chatting with Maria Antonieta, trying to divert the interest this unknown young man has provoked in her. His friends snap their fingers at Junior Meyer to bring him back to reality. Antonio puts his hand on his shoulder and tells him:

—Isn't she a beauty? The most desired young lady of this region and its surroundings.

As they watch the beautiful Marquise.

Junior Meyer has gone mute, Francisco with characteristic lack of tact says:

—An orphan and heiress to a huge fortune!

With warning gestures and almost covering his mouth, Antonio whispers:

—Shshshsh!, don't be so rude.

Meyer does not understand the mystery that surrounds the young Marquise, much less Francisco's words, he just wants to get close to the pretty lady.

Antonio brings him to meet the woman who has stolen his heart with a single glance. She blushes as she sees the gentlemen drawing near and half covers her face with har fan. With confident gestures, Antonio and Francisco greet Martina as foster brothers; Antonio then introduces his friend, the foreigner. Martina has never accepted any pretenders, much less look at anyone as insinuatingly as she looked at Junior Meyer. The resentful women of that society are like poisonous vipers against Martina for the simple fact that she is not yet married at the age of twenty-eight years.

Roderick and Martina are struck by Cupid's arrows from the very moment they set eyes on each other. This day has been one of the happiest in their lives, for both of them. That night is a joyful one for Junior Meyer, who doesn't want it to end, regardless of how sleepy he may be, all he wants is for the night never to end.

He opens his eyes, dreamily awake, laying in that enormous bed, remembering that delicate face, wondering whether she is only a dream or an actual reality?; then they knock on his door and they loudly ask him:

—Erick, Erick! Are you awake yet?

With tired steps he opens the door and, in his German-accented Spanish, switching the "r" for "j" in the pronunciation, answers:

—Come, my friend, come in!, truly, I don't want to wake from this beautiful dream.

Antonio scratches his head and half smiling, confused, says:

—Which dream, man? I'll wait for you in the dining room. Let's go riding for a bit.

Meantime at the beautiful Marquise's house, she sits in front of her mirror where, every morning, one her maids brushes her dark hair, turning into waves that finish in long curls; she drizzles an exquisite jasmine perfume on her neck; she cannot stop thinking about the handsome foreigner and with a seductive smile admires herself in the mirror, making sure the maid doesn't notice.

Her thoughts are lost:

«From where could such a handsome gentleman come from?»

Her maid knows her very well and seeing her so pensive, asks her:

—Mistress! Are you all right?

While Martina continues lost in the memory of the night before. The maid repeats louder, almost yelling:

—My Mistress!

bringing her down from her cloud of love and back to herself. Martina cannot contain her emotions and smiling, takes the hands of the maid in her own. Much more than a maid, she is her confidant, best friend and almost like a sister.

—I'm in love! It's love at first sight.

she says with eyes lit from within by her happiness.

Perplexed, not knowing what to say, Josefa is stunned by the news. Martina shakes off her hands saying:

—Are you really speechless? Come on, say something.

Josefa cannot imagine how, when and where this has happened.

—"Mistress, please, tell me your story of love.

She takes Martina by one arm, bringing her to the old couch, where they spend lazy hours, reading their favorite novels or the poetry anthologies that Martina collects, as she is a hopeless romantic. This time, to learn who was this person that has her mistress in the clouds. They don't feel the hours slip as they talk about it. Martina's dark pupils light up when she tells her the scenes and moments from the previous night. The young men, riding their respective horses, from the hills of those lands with cool seasonal winds, enjoy the beautiful sight and discuss the events from the night before, as well. Antonio, laughing out loud as always, cannot believe his friend, newly arrived in the country, is already in love. Meyer, with his peculiar accent, switching Rs for Js, as if to say don't bother me:

—Since we met, I have not known of any girls in your life. What is the matter with you? Could it be that you enjoy other persuasions?

As Meyer looks at him laughing

This is no laughing matter for Antonio, he is a ladies' man and, like a sailor, believes in "a love in each port". He may have already lost count of how many ladies have been in his life or concept of how many illegitimate children he may have fathered all over the place and with arrogant gestures and his Spanish accent replies:

—I have not wasted the delights that life has offered me but I could never limit myself to just one woman. For your peace of mind, I have always seen Martina like a sister and for your disappointment, I believe she will end up a spinster.

Still laughing, he dismounts and continue:

—Believe it or not, I tell you this because since I can remember, she has not been pretended by anyone.

Caressing his horse's face, the goes on:

—Our parents once had the crazy notion of marrying us but both Martina and I made it very clear that we grew up like siblings and always saw each other that way. Including Francisco.

Meyer hears this and feels rejoiced. Laying

on the grass of that prairie they talk for a long time, especially about Junior Meyer's intentions about the lovely Martina and his desire to buy some land in that Land of Eternal Spring.

He mentions that among last night's guests he met Doctor Jose Mazariegos, rector of the university. He tells him how they talked about the recently founded school of engineering and his offer of a position as a professor. Very excited, tripping over his accent and always switching the sounds of "r" and "j" tells Antonio:

—We agreed on a meeting on Monday, to talk more about this matter.

—That is GREAT news!

Replies Antonio with his own little accent and rising quickly to congratulate his friend who says.

—I really don't have high expectations, I'm a foreigner and I'm sure there will be plenty of competition.

—Even if you 'eat' some words and can't pronounce "R" or "J" I believe you are the ideal person and you will be a professor in the fourth oldest university in the Americas.

His friend tells him patting him on the back. After so many joys, from the center of his heart and his mispronunciations Meyer can't help but say out loud:

—I want to court Martina! I don't want to

lose another minute to see her again, I want to know for sure if she feels the same way I do and if not, set my feet on the ground again, as you have told me.

Surprised, Antonio looks at his friend and jumps onto the horse calling out:

—Say no more... Giddy up, pony, we'll have a wedding soon.

The horse takes off at a gallop and right behind is Junior Meyer, lost in the dust cloud they leave behind. Before arriving at the big house the workers noisily await the unannounced visitors. One of them holds his hat closely against his head as he runs into the house through the back door, the kitchen entrance; he hurriedly enters and sees Josefa, preparing some fruit for her mistress.

—Niña Chepa, niña Chepa!

He calls out and removes his hat; Josefa ask:

—And now what's wrong with you? ¿You look like you saw the devil?

in his broken Spanish, as it is not his mother tongue continues:

—No niña; young master Antonio and a white, white man are on their way here.

Josefa drops the knife as young Antonio, gives her little butterflies in the stomach. She peeks out the large window to spy; her nerves get altered when she sees young Antonio get off the horse with his companion. She rushes into the hall where Martina is and with a nervous voice tells her:

—Mistress, mistress!

—What's the matter, Josefa? Even the dogs are barking.

—Young Antonio has arrived with a white, white man.

Martina rises as if a needle has punctured her thick skirts and runs as quickly as she can to the room, Josefa trailing behind:

—Mistress, wait! What do I do? What do I say?

—Hurry up, hurry up! Please hurry, help me touch up a bit.

Martina did not expect so soon the visit she longed for. Not even twenty-four hours have passed and Junior Meyer and Martina are dying to see each other again.

Little does Josefa understand what happens to Martina over their conversation of the morning but her own nerves betray her just to see young Antonio.

—I have indeed, spread my nerves to you.

Josefa molds Martina's hair hiding her excitement and with a troubled heart sayd:

—Ha!, mistress... I've never before seen you so anxious over a visit from young Antonio?

Betraying a jealous stare over the mirror.

—It's not Antonio and you know it. It's his

friend. Please, come on, my perfume!

Her own hands shake as she grabs the small perfume bottle and she whispers to herself:

«*Easy, Martina, easy! Relax!*».

As she pumps the perfume, looking at herself in the mirror, there's a knock at the door and Josefa goes to open it. A young voice says:

—Niña Chepa!, Young master Antonio and a white, white man are here asking for the mistress.

—She will be down momentarily, serve them something to drink.

Josefa answers to the maid.

Both women head for the reception hall although, out of respect, Josefa walks two steps behind Martina. Both gentlemen rise up and place a hand behind their backs and with the other, take the young ladies' hands and bow down in greeting. Both couples' eyes are connected; Junior Meyer, without blinking, is lost in the dark embrace of Martina's eyes. Antonio wastes no time staring intensely with his hazel eyes into Josefa's tender glance.

Antonio breaks the tension by saying:

—Your house has not changed at all, Marquise.

She restlessly gathers her skirts to sit down and looks at Antonio saying:

—You know I dislike being called that. Sit down, please.

extending her hand in the direction where they should sit.

—And tell me, What do I owe such an impromptu yet pleasant visit?

With a commanding voice and taking over the role of sponsor, Antonio inhales and says his first words:

—Let's call a spade a spade! My friend has fallen in love with you and is here asking for your hand in marriage, dear Martina.

The ladies cough, as if Antonio's voice were laced with chile powder, their throats burning. An awkward pause turns into a tense silence. Josefa is standing next to Martina and seeing her mistress has turned paper-white due to the impact of Antonio's words, without thinking says:

—Young master Antonio, you are always joking.

—I've never been more serious in my whole life.

Martina, with the eyes of a woman in love says:

—Are Antonio's words true?

Looking directly at Junior Meyer's eyes. Without taking his own blue eyes of those dark eyes and with a deep sigh he admits:

—It is true!

She blushes at what she hears and turns to Josefa, almost stuttering:

—My dear!, may I have my fan, please.

Everything has turned uncomfortable, Junior Meyer is nervous, wants the gathering to end, mainly to put Martina at ease. Antonio, is quick to break the ice, jokingly saying:

—So... When is the wedding?, We're not leaving here without a set date.

And laughs out to ease Junior Meyer's anxiety. Martina takes a sip of orangeade as she fans her face with and inhaling deeply tells Meyer:

—I like the last days of the year to start the new one with a new life.

Not expecting a response of that caliber so Junior Meyer rises from his seat and says with a jubilant voice and always with his accent:

—A toast! For the good fortune of not being rejected.

Everybody laughs out loud, easing the restiveness of a few moments ago. Everybody raises their glass of orangeade and toast to the engagement. Antonio shakes off his shirt sleeves with a heroic flair and making a deep bow, says:

—Mission accomplished! Josefita, I believe we must leave the lovebirds alone so that they get to know each other before they marry.

As he giggles and winks at them, takes Josefa by the arm.

The new couple looks at each other, not knowing how to start this new phase of their lives.

—Well, part of my life, I told you yesterday.

Says Meyer without taking his eyes off Martina.

She, also without breaking eye contact with her new beau, replies:

—Not much to tell you about me, I also told you most of my life story yesterday.

As they laugh together, relaxing. Meyer gets up from where he is, he is prepared and putting a hand in his pants pockets, takes out a black velvety box. He gets in front of Martina and gets on his knees, takes her hands and with watery eyes and his mispronounced Spanish expresses:

—For the first time I am in love and for the first time I am engaged; I feel most fortunate it is with Your Grace.

Opens the box and takes out the engagement ring inside, continues:

—This ring was my mother's and I feel very happy to place it in your finger, as the seal to our engagement.

Upon placing the ring, Meyer kisses Martina's soft hand and looking up notices she is flooded in tears. He immediately rises and she steps back to wipe those tears, telling him with a big smile that It's a girl thing, not to worry.

She confesses she has waited for a long time for a moment like this; it's like they already knew each other their whole lives. They're caught up in conversation and don't realize night has arrived as she answers all his questions and curiosity:

—My parents were devastated by the death of many of her friends in that terrible earthquake of September three; my father was very disappointed of the present government and tired of the twists and turns of the liberal revolution; they decided to return to Spain for a little while. I was confident they would be well since Josefa's parents went with them and they were not worried because she stayed with me. However, they were mugged and cruelly murdered on the road, by deserters from the opposition and we both became orphans

As she broke down crying again for this affliction pains her every single day. Meyer consoles her and hands her his handkerchief. She wipes her tears and continues, still sobbing

—Josefa has been like my sister since we were little girls and after our parents' death we're closer than ever; I don't like her calling me 'mistress' but I have not been able to shake that custom off her vocabulary. God knows why things happen but we would have never met if one of us had left with them.

Taking Meyer's hands she continues:

—I did not want to go with them because I love this land so much, I love the cultures of the original peoples, they hide their customs and traditions out of fear of being rejected or worse yet, being murdered. With me they feel free to practice their rites and ceremonies, I will ask their permission to bring you.

Hours have turned into minutes, her eyes are red from crying, she sighs deeply and wipes her tears yet again, realizes it is now dark and calls out with a surprised voice:

—My God! It is night already. Josefa!, Josefa!

And she keeps calling her to bid the gentlemen goodbye.

Antonio has disappeared with Josefa as he has done other times; Josefa knows she cannot expect anything serious with him, he's an inveterate womanizer but she lives and dies for him. She enjoys the moment this Don Juan spends with her, no complications, no expectations. Far away she hears Martina's voice calling her and she quickly dresses and pats down her hair. As Antonio watches and enjoys the sheer beauty of this woman. She is still, looks at him with surprise and getting nervous tells him:

—Don't stay there just laying down! What's wrong with you?, get up! Mistress will be upset.

He is already dressed and remains lost in the sheets just to make her mad; he likes watching her gestures when she is angry and more so when he pretends to ignore her.

Josefa is a natural beauty with long, straight black hair, cinnamon skin, black almond-shaped eyes and a spectacular body hidden under that bulky dress.

The news falls on society like a bomb; the scuttlebutt provides endless entertainment to the ladies with nothing better to do.

Martina could not care less; she is more radiant than ever, is the happiest woman and has vowed to enjoy each moment of happiness that life may give them. Rumors, both good and bad are repeated in the porterhouses and cheap cantinas, where previous pretenders, rejected by the Marquise, try to drown their sorrows.

Junior Meyer gets the professor position and starts teaching the coming school year. The wedding is about to happen and high society scolds:

"The spinster bought herself a marriage with her money and look at the handsome man she got herself! That's what a plenty of bucks can get you".

Josefa is at the market buying all that will be needed for the wedding and realizes how the mocking stares of other young ladies reveal their envy, as she thinks:

«Poor ones!... They will be the ones left on the shelf, for being ugly and fat».

She half smiles looking at them directly and

continues with her errands. She will remain silent without saying anything to her mistress about those rumors. Martina already knows the envy of the women of high society poisons them from within. She looks like a model, tall, elegant, cultured, wealthy and about to marry the most handsome man in the city; the displeasure of those poor, bitter women who cannot shine on their own is to be expected. Rage wounds them like a knife to the breast and all they have to ease their bitterness is to spread rumors.

The bells toll at the great cathedral of Santiago, announcing the grand and unique wedding. Everything is impeccable, lots of white poinsettias and Martina is dazzling in a white dress, white as her soul and a white orchid tiara, handmade by the Mayan spiritual guides, full of blessings.

Antonio and Josefa as godparents hand over the wedding bands, which have been blessed with holy water. The blessings pronounced by the archbishop.

One can smell pine and cinnamon, Christmas Eve is almost here. Just married, they radiate love and happiness which spread to whoever sees them.

Junior Meyer has transferred his entire inheritance to Martina; she has a secret place in her room where she keeps her valuables and keepsakes. Not even Josefa knows of this place, she tells her husband, who has stored his gold ingots there.

Luckily neither one of them needs to work at all, they are financially solvent and they could spend a few lifetimes without worry in that regard; however, Meyer is already hard at work on his first day and since very early. They both have the conviction of leading by example and that's what they want to teach their generation.

Roderick improves his Spanish little by little and gladly shares his knowledge, which has always been his nature. He loves what he does and freely gives it all away, just like his love for his beloved Martina. Knowing he is an archaeology graduate the university offers him a place in one of their expeditions to Peten, a project he would have loved to be part of but had to decline.

They await their first child and he only wants to be next to his wife to enjoy each and every day of her pregnancy. They are so excited about the arrival of the first Meyer-Cabrera.

While Junior Meyer teaches his classes, Martina continues with her social labors, teaching the older workers to read and write. Very few young people and even less children attend her lessons. Some aristocrats don't approve of this, thinking it best to keep the peasants ignorant and illiterate, the same people whose lands they have stolen and distributed to the 'new rich' and the native population placed at the disposal of these allies of the government. Martina suffers over the abuses her people have to endure since there's little she can do for them and what she does accomplish is frowned upon by the nobility. She cares not for the title of Marquise, or her Spanish ascent much less for aristocracy or high society; all she cares about is that a human being be treated as such, since she knows we are all equal in God's eyes. She understands and is very clear in the message preached by Jesus.

Laying in bed as is their custom, the Meyers read before going to sleep. One of those days, they're in the midst of their night reading when Martina notices an old bag hanging from the chair by the desk. Looking at it closely and lifting herself to better appreciate the distracting object, says:

—My love!

—Tell me, my darling!

Says Junior Meyer without taking his eyes off his book.

—That leather bag hanging off the chair...

As she points with her hand at the desk, without realizing her husband is still deep into his reading

—What do you keep there?

Without raising his eyes he answers:

—Love poems that my mother wrote and my Oma's kitchen recipes. My God! How I miss her cooking!

For a moment, raising his eyes and closing the book he stares at the bag, lost in thought.

—May I see?

Says Martina, climbing off the bed and heading for the battered bag.

—Of course, my beloved! Let's see what we find in that old bag.

And he laughs without losing sight of Martina's silhouette, reaching for the bag. With a sigh he admits:

—I haven't opened it at all except to get my parents' photograph.

They take everything in it out and like a curious child, Martina searches all the small tchotchkes and souvenirs until something catches her eye:

—I found a treasure!

She cries out when she picks the locket that used to belong to Junior Meyer's mother, which keeps miniature pictures of his parents and himself when he was a child.

—It's beautiful!

She says... as she opens the little round box, surprised at seeing the pictures inside and taking one hand to her belly, looks at her husband as she happily says:

—I wish for our son to be as cute as this handsome boy!

Laughing Junior Meyer says:

—I'd rather he looks like his gorgeous mother.

As they both laugh and lose themselves in each other's eyes which ends in a deep kiss. Wallowing among the sheets from one side to the other, without letting go, they continue kissing and end up making love. Martina breaks out from her husband's embrace and laughing, sees everything all over the floor; Martina takes one of the handwritten papers and with a melancholy expression says:

—They're written in another language.

—Yes, beloved! They're written in German.

For a moment she remains pensive, reading those papers and with an amused expressions says:

—I'm thinking every evening we should set to translating them.

Meyer raises an eyebrow and, surprised, says:

—All of them?

—At least the recipes, that way at least we can try to make your favorite dishes.

For a moment Meyer travels back to the kitchen of his childhood, where he was so happy.

—Very well, my love! We start tomorrow.

Next day, just as they agreed to the night

before, they started the translation. Junior Meyer writes letters to his dearly remembered Oma; he uses many sheets of paper to tell her everything that he has lived so far and how happy he is next to Martina.

One by one, the German housekeeper's recipes and some of Katherine's poems as well.

Junior Meyer is shocked when, after dinner, he is presented with dessert. His facial expressions range from sheer joy to **nostalgia,** when he sees the container with preserves, he is almost overcome with emotion as he kisses Martina and says thanks to Josefa for the effort in preparing his favorite dessert.

Junior Meyer and Martina do plenty of activities together, without forgetting their individual ones; despite coming from two very different cultures, they are the perfect couple. They have clicked perfectly without hardly any effort at all.

After some time and due to Martina's insistence, Meyer enjoys a rapprochement with the Mayan communities. He is fascinated by all the knowledge they possess. He is stunned by their culture, gastronomy and holistic view of the universe. His studies as an anthropologist and archaeologist are the perfect tool for being able to understand the mystery of the Mayan world. He has the understanding and wisdom to connect with them and they have shared the connection with the sincerity of his heart, which is considered almost identical to that of Martina. His gatherings with the Mayan community happen more often than having tea with the aristocrats. With them he has known the value of life and sanity through nature.

A few days from when Martina will be consecrated as mother, one of the Mayan spiritual guides calls the Meyers with specific instruction about the time, the day and the required elements.

Martina brings all the offerings, exactly as instructed. The ceremony takes place in a secret cave, hidden from the world, since few people understand the power of Mother Nature and Mayan wisdom is unknown by many. The altar is full of flowers, fruits of the season, chocolate, [8] copal, colored candles, especially white, yellow, light blue and green; also, cinnamon, bread, assorted herbs, [9]panela and other ingredients. The fire has begun speaking and is agitated but the message is not encouraging; [10]'Tata' wants to prevent a tragedy but the facts are already inscribed in the book of life.

He gives her a small bundle of herbs and with his broken Spanish gives her these precise few instructions:

---

[8] Copal: Aromatic tree resin, used in place of incense.
[9] Panela: brown sugar loaf, made from unrefined molasses.
[10] Tata: Father

—[11]Nana! Take these herbs home with you and in your hearth, boil them for a while. With that water, fill your bath and stay there for a while. Get dressed without drying off first.

He says goodbye to Martina in a tight embrace and after their farewell, he returns to the altar to continue praying for her, unable to help shedding tears for her.

---

[11] Nan/nana: Mother

MIGRANT DESTINY

SECOND GENERATION

It's September and it looks like heaven itself is falling, raining non stop. Rain sounds like pebbles hitting the roof, wind buzzing and hitting the big heavy doors of the house. The Meyers are in the dining room almost finishing dinner, when suddenly there's a scream:

—Oh dear God!

Martina says as she rises from her seat holding her pregnant belly with her hands. As if he were wearing springs for shoes, Junior Meyer leaps from his seat and is holding his wife in a split second.

She takes his hand and a little frightened says:

—I think it's coming!

Looks at her husband and places a tender kiss on his lips. Immediately they take her to the room, the baby is coming early.

At the Meyer house everyone runs from one side of the house to another. Josefa is in the room with Martina; Meyer can't stop walking back and forth up and down the hallway like a madman.

The minutes seem endless without a sign of the midwife. His beloved's moans are heard through the entire house, resonating together with lightning through the night.

He can't take it anymore and slams the door open; Josefa and the maids are stunned and stare in silence as he kneels by his wife and takes Martina's hand, kisses it and consoles her by saying:

—My eternal beloved! Everything will be alright, please just let me stay by your side.

By her side, he takes her hand and moves to his face to cover it with kisses and caress her face.

One of the workers rushes in dripping water and saying

—The midwife is here!

Roderick feels some relief and the midwife gets close, still dripping water; with a sour expression she points at the door and gestures everyone out of the room. Josefa takes Meyer's hands and tells him:

—Master! Please, let the midwife do her job.

He is crying and accepts Josefa's words, staying right next to the door.

He feels a stab of pain in his chest, a foreboding that something bad is about to happen, cannot contain himself and runs to the patio, where he falls to his knees, raising his hands to heaven, crying as much as it rains, begging for his wife's life and his son's. Soaked through with tears and rain he remains there on the ground. One of the workers takes him back to change and reminds him he cannot let the mistress see him like this.

With every contraction, Martina leaves a little of her life; it is now dawn and she is still in labor. The rainy skies conspire in the mishap. The midwife rubs her forehead and ruthlessly announces:

—The baby is crossed and the woman's age doesn't help... They won't survive!

Meyer launches himself at her throat and with raging eyes looks at her and tells her:

—Save my wife!

Martina does not look good at all and with what little strength she has left, calls her husband over and with a weak voice pronounces:

—Husband of mine! Thank you for all the happiness you gave me until today, I beg you not to say anything against God's designs, it is written in the book of life, just promise me you shall care for our son and will always be the great man that I have loved.

To Josefa:

—Josefa, my sister! Please always care for my son and my husband.

She asks, in a tired voice.

She takes the midwife's arm and squeezing

with her last strength, she begs her:

—Save my son! I don't matter. ¡Save my son!

Martina, making one last effort to save the life of her son, inhales deeply, obeying the midwife's voice who commands:

—Push, PUSH! He's settling.... Almost there...!

There is a pause, a silence. It rains even harder and for a moment, time freezes, not even the rain can overcome the cry of the newborn.

Finally the city doctor has arrived, soaked to the bone.

Martina in her last breath whispers:

—My son... I want to see my son!

the midwife brings him closer and tells her:

—it's a boy!

She holds him close to her breast and kissing his forehead tells him:

—God bless you, my son!

As she extends her hand in her husband's direction, he hasn't stopped crying and with difficulty pronounces her last words:

—Love of mine! I leave you my greatest treasure, now he is all yours. Care for him!

As the doctor checks her vital sign and shaking his head sadly announces:

—I am sorry!

Junior Meyer falls to his knees next to the

bed and cries like a child. He cannot be moved from Martina's side, he's been there two nights and a day, refusing to budge.

Antonio and Francisco finally make him come to his senses. The huge house is full of white chrysanthemums and jasmine, everything smells just like Martina liked it. When they are preparing her for burial, Meyer won't let them remove her wedding band or the locket. He places in her coffin her favorite perfume, his mother's poems and a bunch of gardenias. She is laid to rest in the family cemetery.

That day, the air smells of copal, the Mayan spiritual guides hold a ceremony to honor their dear friend, so that her image endures in the universe's history. Martina, almost at thirty years old, her time arrived.

After the burial, Junior Meyer locks himself in his room, scents every corner of it with Martina's favorite perfume and remains lost in the darkness. He sits in the rocking chair where days before he had caressed her pregnant belly. He is absent, lost in the shadows of loneliness, is like a living dead… He doesn't want to live anymore!

For a few days he hasn't even eaten, despite Josefa preparing daily some of his favorite dishes.

The recipes translated by Martina belong now to Josefa's kitchen, part of the heritage she is amassing.

After a few months, Junior Meyer sinks further into depression until he hears a baby crying. He rushes into the next room, where the cries come from. He enters the room smelling of stale alcohol and immediately Josefa puts the baby in his crib and tells him with concern:

—Master! Your state can harm the child, Heaven Forbid if anything happens to him!

Pushing him out of the room saying:

—Let's go, I'll run you a bath and a strong coffee and that way you can even hold the baby.

As she almost drags him. During the months when Roderick was lost in pain, he hasn't heard from anyone.

Antonio comes to the house to say goodbye. Bad news keeps on coming. He returns to Spain as his grandfather is gravely ill and has requested to see his only grandson. Josefa doesn't even have time to get sad over his departure; she must be strong for her godson Erick and to support her brother-in-law/master.

So many tears, so much pain, many grey days have passed in the life of Junior Meyer but after hearing his son cry the day before, he has risen early and sees a radiant day; all the birds hold a melancholy concert, he sees with new eyes what happens around him.

Josefa stays by the baby's side. If she is in the kitchen, that's where he is. The kitchen always smells of ancestral gastronomy, every now and then mixed with Spanish and German tastes.

But this time it smells like cinnamon and spices and, due to the season, there's many poinsettias around the house.

—Good morning!

Says a manly voice. All those present immediately open a path saying in unison:

—Good morning, master!

As Junior Meyer heads to where little Erick is; with teary eyes, raises the baby and with breaking voice says:

—Forgive me, son, for abandoning you! And not fulfill the promise I made to your mother.

Snuggling him to his chest, still sobbing. Everyone is moved and also cries at the tender scene between father and son. It looks like peace may come again.

Erick! is what they call little Meyer, complying with Martina's wish; his eyes are big and black like his mother's and the Cabrera lineage mole by the upper lip, and the blond hair and milk-white skin of his father.

Young society ladies coyly bet on who will marry the now widowed Meyer, however he does not accept any flirtations he gets everywhere he goes. The love for his beloved Martina still lives within his heart and he complies with the promise made before her tomb, never to lay eyes on another woman.

Junior Meyer is no longer a professor, now dedicates himself to archaeology. He clings to his work to find distraction from the pain he still endures, he knows no rest and travels in expeditions to Peten as often as he can.

Josefa is dedicated to caring for Erick and he fills the emptiness left by the absence of Martina and Antonio.

They celebrate his christening on his first year, it has been a busy day but she is left with the satisfaction of being godmother to little Erick.

They're almost done cleaning when a peasant comes looking for Josefa.

Almost out of breath he tells her:

—Niña Chepa, It's urgent!

As Josefa asks with concern:

—What happened, that you are so frazzled?

—Minga, is about to give birth.

Says with a shrug.

Josefa is surprised, doesn't understand when her parents' goddaughter became pregnant and by whom. What she does know is that Dominga works at Hacienda De la Vega but what she ignores is that she no longer works due to her pregnancy.

Dominga has taken shelter in a hut when she learned she was pregnant, like hiding from the world. When the peasant sees Josefa stunned by the new, he insists saying:

—Minga wants to see you, Niña Chepa. The midwife says she won't make it past today.

—How can this be happening?

She asks as she looks for her shawl and tells Erick's nanny:

—I leave him to you for a moment, I'll be right back.

As she leaves the baby under the care of his nanny, Tomasa, for the very first time.

—Let's go, Juanito! Take me to Minga.

They arrive at the hut where the dying young woman is and with a breath of joy calls out to Josefa:

—Chepa!, Chepa!, thanks so much for coming.

—What happened, Minga? Why didn't you seek me out? Who was the bastard that ruined your life?

So many questions at once daze the young woman but Josefa takes her hands and continues saying:

—Everything will be fine! You'll come out of this one.

Dominga squeezes her hands and very painfully tells her:

—The midwife says that I won't survive, I've suffered a lot with this pregnancy and I was very ashamed, that's why I didn't look for you.

Josefa is indignant for what happened to Dominga and, furious, tells her:

—Who was it, Minga? Tell me!

But Dominga only wants her to listen.

—Let me talk, don't interrupt me.

—Speak, then!

Josefa replies angrily.

The midwife rubs Dominga's abdomen as she tells Josefa what happened.

—That night young master Antonio was piss drunk and came into my room, I couldn't say no. Next day, he didn't even remember what he had done and left for Spain.

Josefa can't stop her tears as she hears Dominga, torn inside that her beloved Antonio could do something like that.

—Chepita!, I have nobody else... you're the only one who can take care of my baby.

—Stop talking rubbish! You will be just fine.

Domiga cries out again:

—¡Chepita!, stop interrupting me, let me talk, I don't have much time...

As the midwife rubs and rubs Dominga's belly and commands her again:

—Push... again... PUSH!

Dominga groans and squeezing Josefa's hands, continues:

—I ask of you to name him after his father, if it's a boy; and if it's a girl, please name her Julia like my mom.

Dominga runs out of time to see her daughter, poor Josefa cries over her body and now has yet another responsibility, one she doesn't know how she is going to face.

They bury Dominga at the Cabreras' private cemetery so that, someday, the little one has a place to visit its mother.

The girl is christened at the village church as Julia Umul, with only her mother's surname. Josefa doesn't wait for Junior Meyer's agreement and while he returns, baby Julia sleeps in the nanny's room. Tomasa, a sturdy woman of Garifuna genes, keeps her hair under a colorful head wrap; she has worked in the Cabreras' big house since the birth of Martina. How tired she is after all these years!

In one of his rest days, when Junior Meyer returns to the big house, Josefa tells him about the little girl; how she accepted the little one without compromising her obligations and responsibilities in the house. Of course, he doesn't see a problem since neither would have Martina and she would have agreed.

Junior Meyer tells Josefa that he has been asked to lead an expedition, as a civil engineer, to the Western part of the country, duration unknown.

—My son will be fine here, I don't want to put him at risk during my trips.

Little Erick is more than used to Josefa's care and remains in her capable hands.

Josefa tells Junior Meyer:

—Master! Go in peace, you know I will care for him more than for my own life.

—I know, I know! The governess will be here next week, I already told her she will care for two children.

—But… master, Julia is still just a baby.

—It doesn't matter, Josefa. Their age difference is only a year, she will be educated right next to my own son. They will not be separated! She's already slept next to Tomasa long enough. When they are a little bit older, they will each have their own room. You should have told me about the christening, I would have given her my last name, Martina would have liked that. But what's done, is done.

Josefa, without saying a word and hanging her head, sheds a few tears.

Junior Meyer, standing by the door, about to leave on his trip, hugs his son tightly, making the sign of the cross just like Martina used to do to him when he left for work, giving her blessing. Little Julia is also loved and receives the same loving care.

The expedition has been working its way up the riverside marking the border for a few months already. Until finally it reaches almost the end of the line. The coach drops camp next to the dividing river.

The place "next to the malacates" impresses Junior Meyer with its tropical climate and dense vegetation, especially, coffee plantations.

On his off days, Meyer rides his horse around the place, filling his blue eyes with the delightful landscape, he really likes that place.

From the bushes, someone watches him; Meyer senses a presence, searching with his eyes, alert in case something jumps out at him. Without knowing if it's an animal or a person, he continues on his way.

They tell of some chilling tales in that place but they make no impression on Junior Meyer.

Rumor has reached the camp that the most feared sorcerer in the region lives around there but they try to ignore the local legends.

Junior Meyer buys a few acres of lands and in his free time has started building a big house. He's called it "Martina" in honor of his departed wife. Construction is well under way, Junior Meyer has taken advantage of the time off allowed by the expedition and invested it in that project.

His days have been exhausting and Roderick has chosen a resting place, appropriate to those sunny days. Almost suffocated by the heat he finds his favorite place under the mango tree. He lays his body under the tree, seeing a blurry shape afar, a man getting close and he immediately rises to meet him, as he is coming right in his direction. The man appears to be in his twenties, medium height, maybe 5' 8" and holding a mysterious staff. Meyer can discern his appearance: ashy skin, with a sparse mustache, somewhat good looking; his head under a red wrap and a peasant's hat, wearing a white cotton shirt, trousers of the same material held with a leather belt, holding a machete scabbard; from his right shoulder a knapsack strap, his feet clad in leather sandals; when he is in front of Junior Meyer, he takes off his hat and with an intense stare greets him:

—Good afternoon, sir!

—Good afternoon, sir!

To which Meyer responds in kind, extending his hand to the man with the gloomy eyes, who does not extend his own and affecting a peasant accent says:

—They tell me you are the new master of these here lands?

Meyer, somewhat uncomfortable with this man's presence, clears his throat and responds in a kind voice:

—People talk a lot. These lands are wonderful and I want to die upon it without being anyone's or anything's master.

The man extends his hand and with a kinder look tells him:

—Demesio Yoc, at God's and your own service, young master.

Junior Meyer, not altogether convinced, shakes his hand:

—Roderick Meyer Jr. also on God's service and your own, whatever it may be, Demesio.

Without further due, the man goes on his way and like a mirage, in the heat, his form disappears.

At full gallop one of the workers helping Meyer in the house's construction asks with a shaky voice:

—Mister, mister! Are you all right?

looking all around.

Meyer, half worried at seeing him so worked up, asks:

—Why the commotion? Did something happen at the work site?

—No, no... sir! We were worried about youse.

—Me? Why?

Asks Meyer with a flabbergasted look and fanning himself with his hat.

—Yes, sir! The man you were talking to is the most feared shaman around here, no one messes with him and rumor has it he's none too happy about building the big house.

Junior Meyer listens with growing incredulity at the worker's words, pats him on the back and half-laughing turns to look at the direction where Demesio left saying:

—Let's get back to work, I gotta go back to camp tomorrow and I wanna have, at least, a place to sleep when I return.

To temper the tension Demesio provoked.

Demesio arrived at his hut, made with his own hands near one of the many creeks in the region. The hut is only a façade for his hideout, he is as mysterious as his stare and inside the hut there is an entrance to a huge cave.

He enters with a frown and hangs his hat on a [12]garabato by the door, heading straight for his altars. Demesio is the last [13]shaman of a long lineage of the [14]Mam ethnicity in the region.

He doesn't understand why this foreigner makes him uneasy. He gathers all the ingredients and herbs and places it all in front of his main altar, he wants to understand the feelings this man evokes. He lights a cigar he made himself, one of those that cause visions and then he showers with [15]cusha, lights a few candles and begins a ritual. His prayers are in Mam, mentioning Tata [16]Maximón quite a bit. The flames ease his anxiety.

Time has run like water between one's fingers and little Erick and Julia grow up together,

---

[12] Garabato: Wooden stick in hook shape
[13] Shaman: Sorcerer. Spiritual leader
[14] Mam: Language and ethnicity
[15] Cusha: Alcoholic beverage
[16] Maximon: Guatemalan syncretic deity

under Josefa's care and protection.

Erick has his father's bearing with his mother's big heart. Little Julia, instead, has a dark skin, as if tanned by the sun, and hazel eyes like her father, her hair straight and black, like her mother's.

The gene mix results in a migrant destiny with mother tongues all but forgotten. In Erick's case he doesn't learn his father's language and loses touch with his German roots; Julia, on the other hand, after her mother's death loses her tongue and, from birth, knows nothing but Castilian. Josefa, anxious for Julia not to lose her identity, takes the children to be presented to the Mayan spiritual guides, to receive their blessing and guidance. She teaches them love for their ancestral roots, just like Martina did when she was alive.

The children learn to love the customs and traditions of this millennial culture and even though they were born to different circumstances, she feels in communion with them.

Josefa teaches Julia all her cooking secrets and the daily running of the house, knowing that she may never perform these tasks but all the same, so that she may direct others to do it for her and do it properly.

Junior Meyer visits his son a few times, his life has become an endless expedition, one after the other. One of the few times he stops by his big city house he mentions to Josefa the lands he's purchased in the Western part of the country.

—The hacienda is called "Martina".

He says with a melancholy voice.

—All I have is for my son.

As he grabs Josefa's hand and continues:

—You've never lacked and you never will, dear Josefa, you are practically Erick and Julia's mother... ¿how can I possibly repay all that you have done for them and for me?

They cry, as they always do when they discuss Martina, they cannot help but be sad and nostalgic. They have long conversations well into the night, until their eyes are lit by the new invention of electric lamps which, by then, have already appeared in city streets and some of the better houses. However, in the Meyer's house, Josefa keeps the candles and oil lamps, refusing to embrace the new gadgets.

Erick, by the time he is ten years of age, promises Julia he will never leave her; soon, his feelings change and from 'best friends' they feel the first tickles of love playing around them; as they get older, they fall in love. Erick and Julia often visit their mothers' graves bringing them bundles of gardenias.

One of those times, Erick takes Julia's hand and in front of them tells her:

—Here, before your mother and mine, I promise you: as soon as I graduate… we will get married!

as Julia, in tears, embraces him.

Erick follows his father's steps, he is just as intelligent and, very young, enrolls in civil engineering school.

From which he graduates with honors! Junior Meyer cannot fail to attend his son's graduation and is present at the party Josefa and Julia have thrown to celebrate handsome Ericks' success.

Roderick is so proud and happy for his son!

As usual, Roderick doesn't fail to bring gardenias to Martina's grave and to tell her about their son's accomplishment.

Erick looks for his father and Josefa tells him she knows where he can find him. He heads for the family cemetery and sees his father kneeling before his mother's grave; he has a different look, not the same sad and bitter visage. Erick, as he gets closer to his father, says:

—Father! I have looked for you all over and Mama Chepa told me I'd find you here, she knows you so well. I have something important to tell you and what better place than here, before our dearly departeds' tombs…

Erick wouldn't call Josefa 'godmother' since, for Julia and him, she is Mama Chepa.

Roderick is surprised by his son's serious

tone and with an anxious voice tells him:

—It must be very important what you want to tell me, my little one. What is it that you want to tell me?

By this point, Roderick speaks excellent Spanish with Guatemalan idioms and no trace of a Spaniard's accent.

Erick inhales deeply and with a strong voice says:

—I've decided to marry Julia!

For Junior Meyer this is not surprising at all, he anticipated it and rose at once to hug his son.

This news greatly pleases him, since he knows his son is and will be very happy with a great woman by his side, almost like his own wife was in her time.

At almost twenty-one years old, Erick begins a new stage in his life, he has decided to share his life with Julia and wants to grow, in every way, by her side.

The wedding is prepared just as Roderick and Martina's; Josefa is very happy and organizes every single detail of the wedding.

Another important event that Junior Meyer cannot miss is that society is deteriorating, racism is rampant and prejudice widespread. It doesn't approve of the wedding.

Erick inherited his mother's courage and his father's bravery, he ignores all rumors. He's conscious some people aim to ruin others' happiness with defamation and discrimination and he knows his own happiness depends on his own decisions rather that whatever people believe and that he will be as happy as his father was with his mother.

Junior Meyer, as a wedding gift, hands them the title to Hacienda Martina.

A few months after the wedding, Julia is pregnant. The news reaches Junior Meyer's ears and he makes all the preparations to return home and be there just in time for the birth of his first grandson.

It is a quiet afternoon, warmer than usual; everyone is enjoying dinner, happy over the recent return of Junior Meyer. Happy… but not a word is heard around the table. Finally, Roderick, breaking the silence around the dining room, grateful for the way in which he was received says:

—Since Martina translated my Oma's recipes, you haven't stopped spoiling me. ¡I am so grateful to you, my dear Josefa!

—Don't say that, master. I only obey to the letter the recommendations of my mistress Martina.

Says Josefa as, with a gesture of alarm, she remembers something… rises from her seat and continues:

—Dear God!, I forgot a letter arrived for you, master. I'll be right back.

Heading to the cedar china cabinet that adorns the dining room, opens a drawer and takes a letter out, handing it over:

—Here you go, master.

—Thanks, Josefa! Oh, it's from my Oma!

Very moved, Junior Meyer opens the letter and as he reads, tears well up in his eyes, falling one by one onto the letter. Everyone looks in amazement as he says with a broken voice:

—My Oma has died!

Erick goes to console his father, knowing the pain he must be feeling.

The sender explains that the housekeeper was his godmother and she has died; she is buried next to Roderick's parents and that he has inherited the big house with a warning that upon the return of the rightful heir, he must give it back.

In that same moment Junior Meyer writes a reply in which he restates to his dear Oma's godson that he has no intention of ever returning to his birthplace and that he can take possession of the property. His only request is for him to take cherry blossoms to his family's tombs, especially that of his mother Katherine Klein.

With this letter, Junior Meyer closes a chapter, the only link remaining that connected him to his native country.

MIGRANT DESTINY

THIRD GENERATION

It will be almost seven at night, dinner almost over, when they hear a scream.

—Ayyyy!

Everyone looks at Julia, who just screamed:

—Holy God!

Says Josefa.

—It 's coming!

Says Julia, soaked with the fluid as her water just broke. She is immediately taken to her room, this time everything is ready a month ahead of time. What happened to Martina was a huge lesson and therefore the midwife has a room next to Julia's, she has cared for her and has stayed by her side in the event of an emergency. Labor has begun and Julia has no contractions. The midwife asks for a tea made of herbs to induce the birth. It's almost eight at night and the sky shines brighter with the light from the stars. Julia groans and moans to push the baby out but she cannot; she inhales deeply and tries again and under the midwife's direction, groans and pushes again and again.

From one moment to another everyone starts screaming, the walls move from side to side and the ground shakes abruptly.

—My God! These nerves are making me feel like everything's moving and I think I'm going to pass out.

Says Erick holding on to his father.

Everything is in darkness, all the lights are out. Stumbling, Josefa reaches into a drawer where she stored some candles, lights one up and gets next to the midwife to shine some light. In the midst of two quakes, Julia was finally able to deliver her baby.

—It's a girl!

Yells the midwife.

Without asking, Erick enters like a speeding bullet and falls to his knees in front of a cross, grateful to God for his wife's and daughter's lives. Roderick cries over his son's happiness even as this scene brings back some of the worst memories of his life, when he lost his wife. Aftershocks are still being felt when, even though it is not the rainy season, a downpour begins.

With the early morning light, everybody's eyes can see substantial damage to the big house. The walls are cracked, some crumbing down, whatever was hanging on them is now on the floor. The news is everywhere; a horrific night, a true cataclysm... We're only alive by a miracle! Is what some declare.

Junior Meyer researched the matter more deeply and sent one of the workers to buy the newspaper, where it says disaster struck the city of Quetzaltenango. Meyer's house has been blessed through the miracle of the arrival of a new member of the family, safe and sound.

Six months later the child was christened as Martina, in honor of her paternal grandmother. The gathering is very intimate, only those closest to the family. After a delicious meal, everyone gathers in the great hall to drink tea and between chats about each person's concerns they discuss how Quetzaltenango and the regions most affected by the earthquake are still no recovered; in the midst of those conversation, they hear loud booms, not knowing where they're coming from. They leave their seats, alarmed, peeking outside trying to see what happens. With concern in their voice and looking out the window, Erick turns to his father:

—What could that be, Father? Could it be a coup d'etat? What we hear sounds like explosions.

Junior Meyer calms his son down and looks out the door, as the evening darkens more due to the amount of ash spewed by the erupting volcano. The eruption has now lasted a few hours and it is impossible to leave. Junior Meyer has had to stay locked in the big house since travel is not possible under the circumstances.

After the volcano's eruption, Meyer returns to his expeditions to Peten, going back and forth as is his custom. His last trip wasn't that long, he had to return shortly. One of the workers comes into the kitchen and tells Josefa that the master is back. She thinks it's strange for him to be back so soon and thinks:

«*How weird, but he just left!*»

Comes out to meet him and sees Roderick looking haggard and, frightened, asks:

—But, master! What's happened?

Junior Meyer, not too happy, replies:

—Miserable mosquitoes have eaten me alive! I've lost my strength, I only stopped for a few things and then I will head to Hacienda Martina, I hope this disease is not contagious and the last thing I want is to infect you around here, especially my granddaughter.

—But... what nonsense are you saying, master?

Josefa is almost crying and helps him into the house, as he says with a tired voice:

—Maybe Martina is coming for me!

With those words he heads to his room. Takes his parents' picture, the one of his wedding and one of his son's with Julia and his granddaughter, Martina. Junior Meyer knows he will end his days at Hacienda Martina and, as usual, only takes with him his most cherished treasure, "his mementoes". He says goodbye from afar, reminding Josefa one more time, to please continue taking care of his family; and with a few workers, he sets off in the biggest coach.

Junior Meyer hasn't visited the hacienda in a few years and thinking his illness is contagious, he instructs only one person to attend to him. It reaches Demesio's ears that the master is back at the big house. Without wasting time he grabs his hat, his staff, hangs the machete from his belt and ties the knapsack around his chest and gets under way for Hacienda Martina. Upon his arrival the servants are surprised and don't know what to do, they're scared; all the villagers fear Tata Demesio. With a commanding voice he asks to see the master. One of the workers heads for Roderick's room and tells him Demesio, the **shaman** is asking for him and Junior Meyer lets him in, knowing who's the visitor. They greet each other warmly and Junior Meyer reminds him of his words when they met, that he wanted to die upon those lands. The rest of the day flies away as they catch up on the events in their lives.

Demesio doesn't say much about himself, there isn't much to tell aside from the mystery of his life. Before retiring for the night, Tata Demesio promises him some remedies to ease his pains but cannot promise to him that he'd save his life, as that is already written in the book of life. Junior Meyer thanks him for his good intentions and continues awaiting his death in that same place.

Every time Demesio visits Junior Meyer, their friendship deepens, time is no object and they enjoy extensive talks. Demesio has never had such enjoyable moments as those he spends with Roderick. Once a week Demesio visits his friend, always with the pot with the promised salve. The servants don't approve of this friendship, rumor has it the warlock is poisoning the master.

Those in charge of watching the area surrounding the property recall the best known tale about Demesio:

A young woman came to him to ask for help to stop her husband from chasing after other women. He made an incantation under the full moon and upon finishing, gave her these directions:

Before each full moon's midnight, she should go out and hunt a hen from which to make a soup the next day to feed the husband, he won't ever look at anybody else. Also warned her to be careful not to be seen... otherwise if something went wrong, she would not return to her human form. By the river shore, under each full moon, the young woman would undress and only leave the belt of her skirts tied to her waist; raising her hands to heaven and saying prayers in Mam, her tongue, she would spin three times and turn into a panther. As soon as she reached her objective, she would return to the river, spin three times again and come back to her human form. One day, her husband noticed that she got up and left in the middle of the night; thinking she went to meet a lover, followed her and hid behind the bushes, watching everything that unfolded. However, when he saw her change, he was overcome by fear but found the strength to run to the river and take her clothes. Hid again and waited behind the bushes, to see what she would do when she came back and didn't find her clothes.

The young woman, returning back to her human state, desperately searched for her clothing; time passed and her husband only watched her. As the clouds slowly covered the light from the full moon, she cried, on her knees, raising her hands to heaven and screaming her prayers in Mam, spun three times again. Looked all around her and with painful roars, disappeared into the night. The husband told everyone what he saw but no one believed him. They said he went mad due to his woman leaving him.

They tell the panther came looking for the shaman to beg him to return her to human shape. He regretted the turn of events and only silenced her mouth to keep her from speaking. He caressed her back and told her the jungle would be her home until the day she died. No one knows what happened to her afterwards… Becoming a legend!

People from that region and its surrounding hamlets keep to many belief systems. The criollos respect religious beliefs and attend mass to make the sign of the cross, to keep the myths away, inasmuch as some do seek the favors of the occult in secret. Of the original peoples few are left but remain faithful to their millennial customs; most of them respect Demesio for he has saved them from death and healed many children. The rest fear him for the same reasons.

Through the hallways of the hacienda house, smoke with a peculiar odor rises from clay containers in order to keep the mosquitoes at bay.

Junior Meyer's condition worsens, he sends one of the workers to get his son, it's time to say goodbye. Erick wants to go alone due to the events happening throughout the country, he doesn't want to risk his family's life, especially since they're not able to use a coach due to the total absence of roads in those faraway lands, but Julia and Josefa insist on going with him, they both want to see Roderick.

The wagon is ready, baby Martina is old enough to travel and can join them. The horses pulling the carriage go at a fast trot, Erick believes they can make it around sunset. With worried faces they travel in silence, things turning dense and boring... only the noise from the wheels and the horses' hooves follows them. Little Martina, at her eight years of age is restless and this trip is no exception; she pulls her mother's hand and with desperation says:

—I need to go to the bathroom!
—What?

Says Julia.

—My God, we need to stop!

Cries Josefa.

Erick asks the coach driver to stop, Josefa says she will help the girl. Dismounting from the carriage she scans the surroundings, searching for a safe space where the girl wouldn't be seen or attacked by an animal. She hugs the girl, brings her down and heads for the place she selected. Josefa spreads her shawl to cover her and checks her pockets for a piece of paper she folded there before leaving. With a laugh, Julia says:

—It's only number one, granny!

Showing one of her little fingers.

—Hurry up, child! Your dad is desperate to make it there!

They all retake the road and when they finally arrive at the hacienda, they're already waiting for them. Erick, without delay, asks with a grieving voice:

—Where's my father?!

One of the workers takes to the room, where he freezes for a few seconds at the entrance, hands around the door frame as if some strange magic held him in place as he sees Roderick Meyer Jr. in his deathbed and with the same magic, he runs to his side almost screaming:

—Father!!!, My dear father!

Junior Meyer's eyes swell with tears upon

seeing his son. With a worn voice and little strength, he want to jump and hold him, stretching his hands says:

—My greatest treasure! The most beautiful part of your mother! Thank you, my son. For coming to bid me farewell... I will soon be together again with your beautiful mother!

Erick kisses his father's hands and minutes later, Josefa arrives with Julia and Martina.

—Master!!!

—Josefa, my faithful Josefa...! Thank you for caring for all of us... I will still ask you to care for them.

—Father!!!

Says Julia from the other side of the bed, flooded in tears.

—My gorgeous daughter! The daughter that life gave to me.

—Thank you, father, for all the love you've given us. May God reward you when you meet Mama Tina again.

Junior looks at Martina, hidden behind Josefa's skirts and still crying, says:

—Mi little Martina, you look the same as your grandmother but the poise of my mother Katherine... I give you my blessing! My precious little Marquise...!

From far they hear like someone is nearing the room. He seems to drag a sentence, walking slowly, to the beat of his staff's sound. One can feel the heavy presence of his bulk, coming down the hallway. The sound stopped at the door and Junior Meyer immediately recognizes him and with effort says:

—t's my friend Demesio!

Demesio removes his hat, his head hanging low, his gaze seemingly lost upon Junior Meyer and with a sad voice says:

—Good night to all of you, present here!

And with the same rhythm that follows him, goes to the foot of the bed, touching his friend's feet and Junior Meyer continues his introduction:

—This is Demesio, with his concoctions has lengthened my life, without pain and has been my spiritual guide; since I arrived here, he hasn't stopped visiting me... My friend! This is my family.

Demesio greets them with reverence and Martina hides her face in Josefa's skirts when Demesio looks at her and a chill runs through her little body.

Meyer pronounces his final words:

—I love you all!

And with an agitated sigh, breaths his last. A wake is held with the hacienda workers and his body is embalmed to make the trip to the big city. Erick is torn apart by his father's death, he never imagined it would hurt so bad; he gathers all his strength to make the return trip and also gathers all the employees. He promises to return soon, tells them his father loved the place and that, on his behalf, he urges them to care for the Hacienda Martina as if it were their own, leaving enough funds for a few years of operation. The expenses will be covered by raising cattle and other farm animals, the harvest of corn and coffee; in charge remains the man who was his father's right-hand man, foreman Pedro.

Demesio, in front of his altars, bitterly cries after the death of Junior Meyer, his soul in pain, one of the few, if not the only person he connected with and one who opened his doors and his heart without prejudice or stereotyping him.

He asks the grandfathers and grandmothers, to the heart of heaven, to the heart of the earth and lights a cigar; he bathes with cusha, lights the candles for the eternal rest of his good friend's soul and makes his own ritual, in his honor, so that he finds the way back to meet his Martina again.

Upon arrival at the big city, Erick holds a mass to honor his father and Junior Meyer's body is buried right next to his wife, Marquise Martina Cabrera. With great cotton clouds the sky seems to draw their silhouettes, holding hands. Their tombs are filled with gardenias and at his sixty-one years of age, Junior Meyer reunites with his beloved wife.

Some time has passed and Erick is still lost in pain, his only distraction his duties as a professor at the university. Junior Meyer did not celebrate his son's birthday as it was a date that reminded him of both life and death. Erick has never celebrated a birthday and on that date he only brings jasmines to his mother's grave.

Two years after Junior Meyer's death, Nana Tomasa passed away too and is buried in the Cabrera family cemetery at her ninety-two years of age.

The years pass quickly like water between one's fingers; the country develops and grows and together with it, its power.

Foreman Pedro has remained in charge and care of Hacienda Martina and one day appears at the door of the Meyers' big house with bad news. He tells Erick how some squatters have built huts on their lands, lands belonging to Hacienda Martina and also, that there is someone interested in buying those lands. The foreman continues telling Erick that, should he not wish to return to Hacienda Martina, it might be a good idea to listen to his proposal, from a man who grows cattle.

With everything that's happened not only inside the country but around the world, now there are rumors of a big war. Nationalist revolts, secret organizations with extreme ideals, the frustrations and tiredness that Erick suffers make him decide to take some time away at Hacienda Martina and once his mind is at ease again, better consider the sale of the lands in question. He tells Julia his plans and tells her they will pretend they're going on vacation while they figure out the sale of the hacienda and soon will be back when that is done; it will only be a few days to help him rest from the pressures and noise of the city. Julia proposes they all go together into the country and that way they will also find some distractions. Erick admits he did not propose it before because he didn't think she would like the idea. Martina is not quite so happy to go with them, his eyes already glow with love for Francisco Rodriguez's son who just returned from Spain just for her fifteenth birthday. Francisco never expected to get so much bad news, since he left for Spain he lost touch with his friends and returned only to sell his properties, his life is well established over there in Spain. He brings with him his eldest son, Francisco Jr. to show him his father's birthplace. He tells Josefa that Antonio is not the same, alcoholism is slowly killing him; after his grandparents died and his parents moved to France, he is all alone. Francisco continues telling Josefa that despite his efforts to help Antonio, he hasn't been able to, as the one who needs to decide to change his life is he, Antonio. All his many offers of help have been rejected and he suffers, too, knowing his friend and almost brother is under the spell of that addiction and there is nothing he can do. Antonio continues like that until he meets his death.

Josefa cries and suffers in silence for Antonio but doesn't say a word. She keeps silent about Julia's existence and if destiny gives her an opportunity to place her before him, maybe then she will be able to tell the truth.

Erick promises Francisco to return soon and asks him to wait for him to accompany him to Spain, he wants to travel with his family and meet Antonio, as his father always told him about how he was one of his best friends, almost a brother to him. With this promise, young Martina agrees to travel one more time to "the boonies" as she calls any place outside the city.

Due to the construction on the new highways, the road is in terrible condition. Erick decided to use the coach again rather than risking a car breakdown halfway there, since foreman Pedro has warned him enough that he knows it would be a very bad decision to drive a car.

The carriage cannot go fast and delays the trip, the road is in worse condition than the last time they traveled it. It's almost nighttime and Pedro asks Erick not to despair, they will be there soon. Young Martina asks for a stop, she needs to attend to some "female needs" just like last time, years ago. Erick is frustrated and before he says anything, Josefa tells him:

—Don't get angry, my child! I will help my young lady Martina.

The only thing Erick can say before Mama Chepa's tender face is:

—Hurry! ¡Let's hope a snake won't get you, you little brat!

They tread lightly behind the bushes and before five minutes have passed they hear the report of an M1898 pistol followed by many continuous shots. Martina rushes out in panic but Josefa grabs her dress, dropping her to the ground; covers her mouth and signals her to be quiet. Martina cries disconsolately. Josefa won't let her go and keeps her mouth covered, telling her they will wait without making a sound.

They've been ambushed by the opposition. The country was beginning to see political murders and they've been confused with one of their targets. They have been riddled with bullets!

Erick is still alive and still makes an effort to get close to Julia's body, begging God for his daughter and hoping she flees, he lies next to his beloved Julia and, by her side, breathes his last.

The bandits, unsatisfied with their murders, set the coach on fire together with the bodies and whatever they could not carry.

One of them says:

—Check the bushes, looks like there was

other people, we can't leave witnesses.

Upon hearing this, Josefa takes Martina's arms and gestures for her to walk to the ravine. They don't know where they are but they find a place to hide. Martina's body is trembling, not knowing if it's due to the cool night or her fright after the events. They remain totally silent until the bandits leave, taking the horses off the carriage.

Martina falls asleep on Josefa's chest, she jumps with shock all through the night while Josefa watches over her sleep. It's the wee hours of the morning when Josefa barely begins to fall asleep when they hear a loud noise and she opens her eyes; she remains motionless, eyes moving side to side but she can only hear the birds singing and the sound of a nearby creek. Looking at her girl, cuddled close to her on her side, with deep tenderness and care, she caresses her hair and removes leaves and debris stuck to her head.

—My girl!

Says Josefa to her ears while frightened Martina jumps up and with agitation asks:

—What happened? My parents! Where are they?

Desperate she starts crawling up the slope which they tumbled down from and which saved them the day before. Josefa holds her up and with a soft voice tries to stop her:

—My girl! Slow down, we don't know what's happened up there, we gotta be careful.

Martina tries to kick off Josefa's holding hands, crying out:

—let me go, granny! I wanna see what happened to my parents!

Josefa, catching her hands, tells her they will go slowly and very carefully.

—Please, my dear girl! Don't be reckless, try to control yourself; we don't know where we are or what happened, we must be careful. Listen to me!

—Right, granny, but understand, these are my parents and I'd die if anything happened to them.

They crawl slowly up the hill; Josefa ahead, sniffing the air like a bloodhound, her eyes like an eagle's, scanning everything around her and at a distance. Josefa feels her hands touch something weird; it's a leather satchel. In it, Erick had the property titles, money and other documents. Erick, when he realized they were under attack, threw it in the ravine. Josefa hangs it across her chest and they continue climbing up, slowly. Reaching the upper edge they see the carriage, still smoking. Martina screams so loudly it scares the birds off the nearby trees, she wants to run to the burnt coach but Josefa holds her back. She hugs her and tries to muffle her loud screams, as they don't know yet what really happened.

They hug each other tightly, kneeling on that desolate stretch of road, cry in grief. After a good while they come back to their senses and slowly begin to grasp what happened. Getting close to the coach, they see the charred bodies and Martina runs to Josefa's arms, flooded in tears screaming:

—Granny!!! Who could do this to my parents? It's so cruel, granny! What will I do without them? Why, granny? I wanna die, granny!

Martina's eyes radiate a stricken amazement before the horrific scene, shaking in Josefa's arms, who can hardly stand on her own feet; her body weighed down by old age and the pain of those she considered her own children, she's about to collapse. Some thoughts cross her stunned mind, she cannot understand such savagery in people. Her crying eyes won't leave the bodies but she reacts and tells Martina they must leave as soon as possible from that macabre place and get help.

Josefa forces Martina to reach and tells her they will follow the side of the road; their look cannot reveal they are from the city. Far away, they see an old man, they speed up to catch up to him. Politely, Josefa asks how far it is to Hacienda Martina. The man tells them which way to take, they're not far, he tells them.

Almost at the entrance to the hacienda, Josefa

looks around, feels someone's eyes and speeds her step up. Martina feels again that sensation she felt when she saw Demesio next to her grandfather's deathbed but says nothing. Hiding in the bushes is Demesio, his eyes deep as the night, are simply dazzled by Martina's beauty. Under her dirty dress and scrapes, with her hair messy and full of dirt, gashes and bruises, he can even see her porcelain skin but cannot tell who she is.

Years of rumors have greatly diminished his prestige with the community and he has become a rough, silent man. One can see the **silver hairs** on his head and his skin worn by time, without losing the demeanor of a strong, decisive man.

After Junior Meyer's death, Demesio had not shown himself around Hacienda Martina. Despite her years, Josefa finds the strength to hold on to Martina. The young woman's heart can be heard like an overwhelmed drum and almost out of breath tells her:

—Stop, granny! I feel like I'm passing out.

—We're almost there, don't give up; look, my girl, we see something over there.

Among the bushes, Demesio still stalks them, like a hungry wolf, following their every step and Josefa turns to look at the bushes and for a moment he fears the old woman has seen him. The great entrance is deserted, they see the name Martina, hanging from a corner and they find some relief in having arrived. Completely worn and almost out of strength they collapse at the hallway. From an old shack a sentry appears, with an angry face and he starts shoving and pushing them. Finding strength, Josefa warns him he will regret treating them this way. Incredulous, he shoves them harder and Martina, having had enough of his attitude tells him with authority:

—I am Martina Meyer, I was eight years old when I came with my father, the day my grandfather died.

Ashamed, he apologizes and helps them into the house.

Well into the afternoon, they arrive at the house. Josefa tells them the horrendous experience they just had. ¡What a tragedy! Josefa sends men to recover whatever remains they can gather to properly bury them.

Demesio returns to his hut and enters, with a feeling of desperation, the cave. He wants to consult with the grandfathers and grandmother, to answer for this strange feeling that stifles him and one he cannot figure out… he wants to understand this overwhelming feeling the young woman creates in him. The answer was very clear but he disobeys the reply he gets from the flames. He uses his gift without permission and creates his best hex, at the same time dooming his own life and that of his descendants up to the third or fourth generation.

He leaves the hut as he always has, hoping to find love although he thinks he found it the day before. His eyes shine now, now he wants to change destiny. He visits Hacienda Martina again, remembering the good times he had there in the company of his good friend, when he was alive, even though he forgot some details about the big house since then. His walking style only changed because his steps are slower now; his bearing is the same. He asks the first worker he finds for the women he saw arrive at the place and not leave again. The worker doesn't answer but rushes back to tell Josefa about the man, for his sole presence fills with fear those who see him. He is immediately taken before Josefa and Demesio momentarily forgets who the women are, he only wants to see the young woman.

Josefa remembers him and makes a reverent bow, as the Tata he is, kissing his hand and thanking him for his presence. She tells him what happened without knowing that Demesio is there with quite different intentions, he is blinded with lust for Martina.

He asks to see her, she is bedriddem dehydrated, without strength. Upon seeing her, he inhales deeply and exhales with a sigh, so strong it shakes the young woman's body and before she wakes he leaves the room. He takes a bottle out of his sack, covered with a corn cob, where he has the concoction for his hex. He leaves instructions with Josefa, like a doctor would, and disappears like a phantom.

The city newspapers publish the news: "The coach in which the Meyer family travelled was robbed and burned, there were no survivors". When Francisco reads the news he cannot believe so many tragedies befell his friends. The only thing keeping him in the country is the pending return of the Meyer family for the trip to Spain they agreed to. Without waiting to find out more about the murders he returns to Spain, very frightened for the rampant violence in the country.

The government takes over the entire Meyer estate and the peasants are thrown out and stripped off the lands Martina and Junior Meyer legally granted them.

Greed has no mercy once the land grab takes hold, the titles are changed and those most in need are left bereft and to their own devices, in disgrace. Josefa is worried that no one from the city shows up at Hacienda Martina, after she has sent many messages. She cannot understand why they've been abandoned by the family's friends; not even Francisco, whom she knows is awaiting them, has shown up. Little does she know Demesio is responsible; any opportunity for anyone to separate him from Martina's love. She recovers little by little, calling Josefa without knowing her will already belongs to Demesio. She takes Josefa's hands and with listless eyes asks:

—Granny Chepa! Where is Demesio?

—Why do you ask for that man? You haven't even noticed when he comes to heal you.

—I have noticed, granny, and I've seen his love when he cares for me and I don't want him to leave my side.

Josefa is bewildered by Martina's decision, it's like another person speaks for her. No human power can make her change her mind, Josefa wants to understand, ¿what happened to her little girl? She knows very well from the first day she met Francisco's son, she fell in love with him. Josefa wants to understand when those feelings changed. Upon Demesio's arrival, Josefa looks him up and down and with angry eyes and almost yelling, says these words:

—I have respected you since I met you, because spiritual guides, good Tatas deserve it... but tell me tata, what happened to the friendship my master gave to you? Do you not see your age and that she is a little girl? She is infatuated like any young girl... You put a spell on her! This is how you repay the love and respect we gave you? I don't believe the grandfathers and grandmothers approve of what you do. Free my girl from your spells, let her live, give her back her free will!

He is stunned and silent, hits the ground with his staff and pierces Josefa with his black eyes and without the slightest remorse tells her:

—It is done!

Leaving Josefa under warning he goes on to Martina's room. Josefa felt paralyzed for a while and said no more about the matter. After a few days, Josefa, unable to speak, tells Martina they must return to the city. Martina's hazel eyes are glinting strangely and tells Josefa she is not going back. Her only desire is to marry Demesio. This decision almost gives Josefa a heart attack. The marriage is consummated on a gray day, as if signaling the universe's deep disapproval.

The girl becomes a woman, and Josefa cries night and day, unable to protect her girl from his demonic claws. On her knees she begs for forgiveness from her ancestors, she doesn't know what to do before this odious sentence which took over whom she considered her granddaughter. Little by little, the hacienda falls apart; with Demesio as the master, the workers are scared away and they leave, one by one. Josefa wants to scream and make Martina wake up from this nightmare but, unable to get through with words, writes her notes, without Martina ever reading any of the messages.

In a few months, the air feels heavy,

Demesio's eyes are everywhere. Christmas came and went without notice in the big house, it passed like any other day and Josefa only knows it's New Year's Day because of some distant noise. She gestures to make herself understood, as if wanting to know what is happening and the only remaining worker tells her it's the New Year. Josefa still cannot believe all that happened in such a short time; she begs God to give her strength and just a bit more life, to rescue her little girl from that terrible monster's hands, for that is what Demesio has become.

It's the age when suffering souls won't let those alive live and legends become credible. The beautiful Martina appears to be sleepwalking, her belly swollen and no joy on her face. Josefa walks ever more slowly, the years of hard work tire her daily, only the love for her girl has kept her alive. Death is rampant all over the world in a massive epidemic; the dead lie in rows on the sidewalks, awaiting the forgiveness of their sins. Some say it's the end of the world.

Martina turns sixteen and it's a day only Josefa remembers. With the few utensils left in the kitchen and whatever ingredients she can find, she prepares a delicious luncheon for the girl.

All workers have left Hacienda Martina, there's no one to attend to the daily work and in a few months it has become a pigsty.

Josefa makes an effort to cook some food, wash the clothes and tend to her girl.

MIGRANT DESTINY

FOURTH GENERATION

In a dark and dank room, full of detritus and not very clean, Martina goes into labor. Josefa, desperate, tells Demesio through signs that the girl needs a doctor or at least a midwife. The only thing she gets back is an intimidating and threatening look from Demesio, who seems to care nothing for Martina's life, much less her baby. With his sour face and deep voice he orders Josefa to get some hot water and clean rags.

He has everything ready to attend to the birth of the baby. It's not the first time he does it, he's been a healer to the villagers and, since there's never been a midwife, Demesio has tended to the births in the surrounding areas. Josefa only prays to God that Martina's and the baby's life be saved. The miracle surprises Josefa and Demesio himself when they realize Martina gives birth immediately and without complications. Maybe it was her youth or destiny marking a new beginning. Demesio washes and cleans the baby, swaddles

her in a cotton blanket and hands her over to Martina, to whom he says without any joy:
—It's a female!
And leaves the room.
Martina takes the baby in her arms and caressing her silky head, says:
—You will be my reason for living and you'll be named Julia, in honor of my mother.
Holds her against her chest and when feeling her little heartbeat, it's like she awakens from a nightmare. She extends her hand to Josefa and sighing deeply tells her:
—Granny! Get close, look…. She's like a little doll.
Josefa is flooded in tears
—Don't cry Granny Chepa! After so many tragedies, she has come to alleviate so much suffering.
Josefa kisses Martina's hands and holds the newborn in her arms. Seems like everything is back to normal and in one of the few lucid moments Martina has, Josefa makes one last effort to persuade her and writes:
"Do not take any remedy from Demesio".
Young Martina doesn't understand why her granny Chepa writes those words but obeys her. Little by little, the concoctions have dwindled and Martina's mind starts reasoning again. She ties the loose threads and starts feeling a strong

revulsion against Demesio.

With whatever little is left in the hacienda, the neglect and the damage caused by the last earthquake, Martina slowly starts shaping a home. Clarity and cool arrive. Josefa is really worn out and with whatever little strength she has, she helps Martina clean and deodorize the recoverable spaces. Josefa is only awaiting for her death but projects strength before Martina and gives her courage.

Before anything else happens, she writes her last letter:

Hacienda Martina, September 2nd, 1918.

Dear granddaughter of my heart:

Maybe when you read these words, I'll be dead already. I don't write to scare you, I know you're strong as were, in life, your grandmother Martina and your grandfather Roderick; you are brave as were your mother Julia and father, Erick.

I write to tell you I love you with all my heart and you've been the apple of my eye, just like your parents were, before you.

Don't forget what we told you; practice the recipes we used to make with your mom, grandmother's recipes. Tell your daughter our history and that of your ancestors, don't let our memory die as well.

Don't let Demesio's dark shadow overshadow your own light. Pass your knowledge on to your children, if you have any more. Blood is kept alive through our customs and traditions; let the memory of your heritage prevail from one generation to the other.

Your father's leather satchel is under my bed, I moved some boards on the floor and opened a hole, where I hid it. It contains the title to the property and some money. Demesio was a good man, I don't know what made him so evil. Don't provoke him and just stay safe so that you can protect your daughter.

I bid you farewell,

Granny Chepa.

On finishing the letter, Josefa tries to keep it close in order to give it to Martina at the right moment.

When it rains in that part of the country, it's a torrent, with thunder and lightning and it doesn't stop for days on end. Buckets are not enough to prevent the inside of the big house from turning into a river.

Martina starts recovering her elegance and courage; the shaman's lasted a few months, when she, in a few lucid moments, brightens her face with a smile. Demesio visits his hut every now and then, that's where he keeps all his ingredients and recharges his energies. He is burdened by the distance with Martina, as much as she tends to him in all wifely duties, except the intimate.

    Josefa tries not to run into Demesio, not in the hallways or the kitchen; the few times they coincide, he makes her sick to her stomach. One day she decides to write a letter to Demesio.

Señor Demesio:

I beg of you, for the sake of the memory of my master Roderick and his son Erick, please, set Martina free of your black magic.

    She keeps the note in a pocket of her dress, to give to him whenever they coincide. She sees him come down the hall and this time, she doesn't retreat, she stands in front of him. Signals him to stop, takes the paper out of her pocket and gestures him to read. Demesio, with an angry face, takes the paper and starts tearing it, without stopping says, furious:

—I don't know how to read or write!

And storms away into a room.

    Little Julia turns six months old; her eyes dark like coffee, she watches the women in the kitchen. She knows they're preparing the mashed potatoes she likes so much. Josefa supports herself with the rustic table in the middle of the kitchen and slowly looks for a place to sit but she drops onto an old chair, close to baby Julia. Martina can't help her anguish and screams:

—Granny Chepa! What's wrong?

—It's time to join my dead ancestors, my child, don't be sad.

With a slow and shaky hand, she searches in her pocket for the letter she wrote for her, it's the perfect time. Martina yells for the young girl Demesio brought as help with the chores. Julia cries, scared, not understanding what is happening.

It wasn't the plague or the flu, not even malaria, which ends Josefa's life. Her strength has been slowly depleted. Sadness over her dead ancestors, the pain of seeing her little girl possessed by the evil Demesio, she held everything inside and in silence. Fatigue has won the battle and with great effort, she leaves her blessing for her little marquises.

Martina cries until dawn, next to the corpse of her dear granny Chepa. Her tears cleanse her soul and the pain she feels over the loss of Josefa only makes her stronger.

She buries her next to Erick and Julia. Josefa rests in peace at her seventy years. Martina plants carnations around their graves.

Demesio doesn't show himself at the house

for many days. Martina doesn't miss him at all, her full attention is dedicated to little Julia. Martina starts a small business, selling apple and cherry preserves, beginning to put into practice all the teachings of Josefa and Julia. At her young age she learns to be independent and brave. She carries her daughter like the peasant women do and walks to the village to sell her preserves. Because of her bearing, they call her "the foreigner"; they've never made the connection she is the shaman's wife. Every time she comes to the village she buys the newspaper to stay up to date on the events of the moment. One of those times, she looks for the paper at the usual place and asks whether it has been sold out? She cannot find a single one. The storekeeper tells her they are no longer in circulation; the printing presses have been confiscated by the government, which suppresses journalism and free speech.

Julia grows up as gorgeous as the lineage of her grandmothers. She can hold a pencil already at three years of age; Martina teaches her to read and write at an early age. She wants her child to be educated, just like she was. Julia is shaping up to be a warrior, like her mother, with the gifts of her father.

Demesio is desolate over his beloved's

rejection, he hides in his hut and drinks all the [17] guaro he can. He returns to the big house, straight to Martina's room and roughly grabs her. She doesn't resist or make any noise, hoping to keep her little daughter from noticing and from the violation of her mother.

The next day Martina gathers her courage and faces him; with a strong voice and machete in hand, she gets in his face and tells him:

—Don Demesio Yoc...! I don't know what filth you've given me and what powers you use to keep me by your side; but from this moment on you will never defile my body again. I will be here until the day I die but you will NEVER be close to me; the day you even try, you will be a dead man.

Demesio is perplexed at seeing the machete, raised in Martina's hand. Not his concoctions or his witch power can stop Martina from defending herself like a lioness and from that day on, he only shows up to eat.

Every night Martina takes her little daughter to bed and before she falls asleep tells her stories of her grandparents. Even though she doesn't know if the five year old girl can understand, she also instructs her on what to do, should she not be by her side someday. She repeats it time and again, night after night, the same tales. Martina uses every minute of the day to teach Julia how to

---

[17] Guaro: cheap "aguardiente" liquor

survive on her own. It's like she has a foreboding that her own life will soon be extinguished and she worries because her daughter is still very little.

The only two times Demesio has been intimate with Martina, he's made her pregnant and son she is feeling labor pains again. Demesio is by her side, attending to the second birth, he doesn't even open his mouth and only Martina's moans are heard. After not too long, the cries of a baby are heard. Demesio was hoping for a boy and the disgust is evident as he whispers:

—What a disgrace, another female!

Without another word, he leaves the baby on Martina's boy and loses himself in the dark of the night. The woman who follows Martina all around, cleans her up and gives her a cup of tea, which Martina looks at with mistrust. Maria de Jesús sees her and with a peasant accent warns her:

—Drink it, mistress! I made it myself, it's a remedy my mother taught me, she says it's good for healing inside women who just had babies.

Martina takes it and, still unbelieving, takes a couple of sips and immediately asks for little Julia. Chus, as they call the woman, tells her that the girl is asleep and not to worry about her, she has cared for her exactly as told... to the letter. Once she has her newborn in her arms, she looks at her and caresses her little head. Smiles at her and with a soft voice tells her:

—My little one! As beautiful as my great-grandmother Katharine, whom I did not meet but I saw her in the photograph my grandfather kept next to my great-grandfather... We look so much like her.

Laughing and crying at the same time, she continues caressing the little baby and tells her:

—How our lives changed from one moment to another! But I'm here for you, daughter of mine, strong! For your sister and for you. You are my reason for living and I will recover our history. You will be named Victoria, because you were my strength and gave me courage to put an end to your father's abuse.

Now Martina has twice the responsibilities, but she doesn't give up. Each day she has a new idea and La Chus has become her right hand. Twice a week, Chus goes to the village market to sell their preserves and buy supplies. Apples and cherries are not always in season but, lacking those two ingredients, Martina replaces them with mangoes and [18]jocotes. They are plentiful in this area, especially in their own lands.

The recipe she uses is the same that she learned from her mother, Julia, and Josefa and they both followed the recipe from Roderick's

---

[18] Jocotes: is a small tropical fruit, It is a popular fruit throughout Central America, particularly in Guatemala.

housekeeper, his "dear Oma". The preserves are a hit and demand grows. Every time Martina makes those preserves or any other recipe she was taught, brings back to her memory the stories her granny Chepa told or her mother Julia laughing out loud in the huge kitchen of the big house, in the big city. She wants to keep those memories alive!

Each recipe she makes, whether a preserve or any other dish, with happy faces, she teaches it to her daughter Julia. The little girl, at eight years of age, already knows how to make all her mother's recipes and learns very quickly whatever she is taught.

Near the big house there is a creek and Martina, with great ingenuity, shares wonderful picnics with her daughters. Stone by stone, around an area with the most water, she makes a small pool, the children delighted at their mother's creativity. As Martina watches her daughters, she notices how much the water moves when close to the banks of the small river. She gets closer, slowly, to see why. She notices many small caves, from where the reason for the water's movements comes.

She finds the bucket where she carries fruit for the girls, removes her head wrap and catches the first [19]juilín with many more hiding inside the

---

[19] Juilín : Type of small freshwater fish

caves. Then Martina feels something strange against her feet and stands still for a moment; the depth at the riverbank is not more than her ankle; slowly and with the same head wrap she touches down and when she takes her hand out of the water, she is so happy she yells:

—Shrimp!!!

She hasn't seen them in a long while and now she can bring them to her table for free. She's very happy because this expands the range of foods they eat. Most of the foods that come to her table are grown by her as well as raising fowl. Her intelligence, knowledge and creativity have all been put in practice to make sure her daughters don't lack for anything. She makes a net for fishing [20]juilines and shrimp. Little Julia helps her mom and one of those times, notices something hidden in the rocks, calling for Martina to see what it is. Carefully, Martina moves a rock and finds a black shell with large pincers, ready for the attack. Even more carefully she catches it and realizes the small river also contains crab. When it is their season, they take advantage to hunt them

Martina cooks the fish, shrimp and crab in many different ways. They just returned with some shrimp and Martina is in the kitchen, making a delicious dish. The girls are around her and she tells La Chus:

---

[20] **Juilines:** small freshwater fish; catfish fry.

—Chusita! Go cut some [21]culantro, mint and lemons, please. I already have the other ingredients.

Julia's curiosity doesn't take long and she asks her mother:

—What are we making, mommy? Why are you chopping the shrimp?

In reply to her daughter's questions, Martina says:

—Hand me the tomatoes and onions… you'll see what a delicious mix we will make! We will dice everything very finely, but first we cook the shrimp with plenty of lemon juice and then we mix everything; we leave it to marinate a good while and then we season it with salt and pepper. Just in time after Chus makes the tortillas, then we'll taste it. Separately, I will also finely dice some [22]chiltepes and whoever likes some heat, can add it.

—Mmmmm…. Mommy! My mouth is watering!

And with a boss' voice commands Chus:

—Hurry up, Chus, to make the tortillas!

The [23]poyo is always smoking hot and Martina ensures it doesn't lack firewood,

---

[21] Culantro: Cilantro
[22] Chiltepe: a variety of a small chile, also known as "piquin" in countries such as Mexico.
[23] Poyo: home hearth, uses firewood such as "chiriviscos".

otherwise telling the girls they're going on a walk. The beautiful hike they follow is a circle of the property, looking for [24]chiriviscos, seasonal fruits and telling them tales of their family. That's how she has kept them happy and the home fire burning, always ready for cooking a delicious meal.

Martina thanks God every meal time for never failing to provide them with sustenance. She's been able to keep her daughters healthy and to teach them the good customs she was taught. Julia and Victoria are learning to be grateful.

Chus is in charge of making tortillas, grinding the [25]nixtamal in the maize grinding stone, preparing little balls of masa and shaping them by hand into the tortillas that end up on the enormous clay [26]comal. Julia has also learned to make them. She loves learning!

In the hearth there's a clay jar, worn from continuous use; in it, the coffee that Martina has prepared is boiled first and then strained through a cloth.

The few coffee and cacao bushes still remaining in the hacienda have been rescued by

---

[24] Chiriviscos: dried branches and twigs.
[25] Nixtamal: Corn boiled together with lime prior to grinding it into "masa". Masa: dough made of ground corn and water.
[26] Comal: A large clay plate placed on the flames of the heart, where tortillas are made.

Martina from neglect and it's the ones providing her with the delicious coffee that perfumes the house in the morning, fragrance that turns to chocolate in the evenings.

All the activities Martina does with her daughters, she makes them fun. From cutting coffee through every one of the steps that follow. Same with cacao. Between laughter and games, the girls are learning, especially Julia, who is a keen observer and asks questions about everything she doesn't understand. Martina has infused them with a sense of security.

In those trips to the village she bought a beat-up coffee grinder that eliminated the chore of doing it with a stone grinder.

Seems like life is taking a new course. Martina even forgot to return to the city, she has found her own happiness with her daughters and would rather not risk Demesio doing evil to them. She hardly ever sees the perfidious Demesio and she thinks everything is fine but that man has a thorn in his side and he wants it pulled out somehow.

The fact that she ignores him is his daily torment and in the shadows he plots something malignant. Daily, Martina teaches the girls to prepare themselves mentally and physically, as if she senses she won't always be there to protect them. Before the little ones go to sleep, as if telling them a bedtime story, they pay close attention to her voice and gestures as she tells them:

—My girls! No one has the right to harm you and neither do you to harm someone else; however, if anybody dares try, with your own teeth and nails, you must fight to save yourselves.

In telling her tales, she roars like a cat and the children jump in fright as Martina throws herself on the bed to tickle them. In laughter and games, they go to sleep, exhausted, not without thanking God before, for another day of life. Julia is ready and knows what to do in the event of any incident.

From afar, Demesio watches Martina's every move and in his ignorance, he dislikes it all, doesn't support her and does everything he can against her. His mockery doesn't really offend Martina; he keeps telling her she will never be accepted in high society and to resign herself once and for all to live there and leave all her customs behind. She knows she will never recover what is hers, by inheritance from her parents and has no idea what happened with their properties in the big city. For Martina, Demesio's words are hollow and she ignores them just like everything else he tries against her. She doesn't know what may happen down the line, all she can do is enjoy life with her little ones and she's completely forgotten about the outside world. She created a different world for her daughters and prepares them day after day. She wants them to have her legacy!

Demesio is furious since Martina isn't hurt by his offenses and knowing that if he touches her again, he is a dead man. He dies slowly seeing as Martina gets more beautiful and full of life by the day and he, a bitter man, also grows older by the day.

As usual Martina stands by the river shore with the girls and Demesio comes just to argue with her. Only she pays him no attention. He is so angry he goes into his hut in a rage. Once more he locks himself in for days in the cave, dusts off the old ingredients and herbs, uses his evil powers and once again disobeys without any attention to the consequences. He is in such mortal pain that, in desperation, he performs a death ritual. The wear and tear from it left him laid on the floor for a couple of days, after which he wakes up from the trance and cries over his dishonor before the grandfathers and grandmothers.

It's a resplendent day and Martina tells Chus it is a good day to do laundry. They take the clothes to the river since Martina built a buddle and it's much easier to wash clothes there than in the stone washer her grandfather built by the well. On the long strings tied from one tree to another, they hang the clothes. As dusk nears, Martina doesn't want the girls outside and orders Chus to take them to the kitchen and get started with dinner. She picks the clothes from their hanging place. The day is still brilliant, the kind that doesn't last long in this region. Suddenly a thunder is heard, loud as a bomb. Martina looks all around her and notices near her a round burnt spot on the ground and raises her eyes to the sky and sighs deeply, saying:

—Ayyy, Holy Heaven! A dry lightning and like La Chus says... when there's no sign of rain... it's the sign. My God! I am ready.

Martina still folds the clothes and as she prepares dinner feels a deep pain in her chest, without paying attention, so that nobody notices.

They have gone into the room earlier than usual and she tells Julia:

—My big girl, Julia! Do you remember all that we've been talking about? If something happens to me, you know where the money is?"

Jullia with teary eyes responds:

—Yes, mommy! I know everything.

Martina continues refreshing Julia's memory... without tears:

—You're going to take care of little Victoria, I've also given some instructions to La Chus but only a few, something about her still doesn't convince me. Be very careful with her! I already told her where to buy the bread and coffee, if needed. Don't cry my precious Julia, you'll be as strong as you have been until now, I know you are still little but I also know you've understood me to the letter. I promise you that wherever I may be I will take care of you two, maybe from heaven; just like my own ancestors did with me.

Sobbing and understanding what was about to happen Julia can only say:

—yes, mommy!

Without understanding the conversation, Victoria also repeats:

—Yes, mommy!

Martina hugs them tightly against her and tells them:

—I love you with all my soul!

Julia starts crying and holding her mother tightly as well tells her:

—Everything you've taught me I've learned but please don't leave me, mommy, never leave me, please.

Victoria is scared by her sister's cries and joins her, too.

Martina hugs them again and tells them:

—Don't cry my lovely little marquises! Today we won't have reading or storytelling; I feel very tired and I wanna go to bed earlier, let's pray and sleep, tomorrow will be another day.

The oil lamps go out and everything is in darkness. Exactly at midnight, Julia wakes up frightened, as if presaging her mother's death and runs to wake up Chus, shaking her with desperation telling her:

—I wanna see my mommy!

Half asleep, the servant lights the oil lamp and they head for Martina's room as La Chus says:

—Sshhhh! She's asleep, we mustn't wake her up.

But Julia runs to the bedside. Martina's body is lifeless and Julia shakes her mother, yelling:

—Mommy, wake up!

She continues shaking Martina's boy and when she doesn't wake she starts screaming:

—Mommy, don't leave me! Please don't leave meee!! What am I gonna do without you??

La Chus lights all the oil lamps and starts blowing on the embers still smoking in the hearth, to make coffee.

Demesio comes in the middle of the night, stunned in his sleeplessness. From afar, before getting to the house, he sees all the lights are on and knows right away something bad has happened. In Martina's room, Julia, laying on top of her mother, fell asleep after crying so much. The following morning, Julia lashes out her anger and sadness, uprooting the corn she planted with her mother. They were just starting to grow, like Martina's life, cut short at twenty-four years old. After losing herself among the crops, flooded in tears, she holds her mother's wake, just as she instructed her. Martina has been buried right next to her parents and her beloved Granny Chepa.

The story takes a sudden turn; not only in Julia's and her sister Victoria's life but for the whole country. Two people in different fields of life cease to exist under suspicious circumstances. Martina's death, as mysterious as Demesio himself and the strange heart attack that took the country's highest authority, putting an end to the illustrious leader [some believe he was poisoned].

Demesio seeks shelter in an old and abandoned hut, falls to his knees before the altars. He screams for forgiveness! But the fire doesn't answer. He's stayed there working hard to recover his legacy before the eyes of the grandfathers and grandmothers. He knows disobedience brings horrible disgrace and dooms his descendants for four generations. The firstborn are already marked!

Julia takes the reins of the house and puts into practice the teachings of her mother, since she is responsible for little Victoria. La Chus starts changing her attitude, she dislikes getting orders from Julia. Julia remembers her mother's words and tries to avoid her but there is very little that she can do, an eight year old child.

After months shut in his cave, Demesio returns to the house. Julia rejoices, thinking things are improving with Chus but her father returns more arrogant than ever, ordering them around like the master and lord of the house! He's taken over his deceased wife's lands.

Martina improved the hacienda a lot and at least some of the workers were available to her when she needed help for heavy labor but they have all abandoned the hacienda knowing Demesio is the new boss.

Two stormy years have passed for the girls and Demesio decides to get together with Chus and they start living together. He doesn't care if his daughters suffer continued abuse at her hands, he just wants to erase the memory of Martina. What little authority Julia had is taken away by Demesio, who gives it to Chus and this worsens the suffering for Julia and Victoria.

With Chus, Demesio finally has the son he wanted so badly to have with Martina. He names him Victor, a name Martina had chosen in case she ever had a boy. Victor is born blind and while he is not Demesio's first born he is Chus', thus his tragedy. La Chus had two more births and they are both female. Her daughters grow up just like her.

Destiny should work very hard to give peace back to Martina's daughters.

There is no harmony in the house, the fights are more frequent between Julia and Chus.

Demesio remains shut-in among candles and copal, alien to the girls' harsh reality. The servant has become the step-mother and ignorance blocks the future of this generation.

Julia cooks for the little sister and continues making preserves. She takes them to a bakery where they resell them, she didn't need to sell them at the market. She won't leave her sister at the mercy of the step-mother, wherever she goes, she keeps her close by. Her father did not return to the cave. He burned the hut and moved into the big house.

That's where people come to see him, for the jobs he still does, he is good at it and people won't stop seeking him out. Julia avoids running into him, for he has insisted in teaching her his craft and she refuses to learn but there's no need to teach her, she has it in her blood, like any firstborn of Demesio's lineage. They are also doomed due to the debt he has before divinity.

Julia is growing up very quickly, she is quite a young lady, looking like the Cabrera line. According to her understanding of what they have been through, she grows more disappointed with her father. It grows when she sees how, little by little, he liquidates the land that belonged to her great-grandfather and thus belongs to her and her sister. However, Julia doesn't say anything and respects her father's decision since, as Martina's legitimate husband, they are legally his.

The area grows in population with new landowners and they have cut down the giant trees which helped cool the place down, the heat is now suffocating. Upon seeing the growth in the region and how her father wastes the money from the sale of land, she hustles for her own money so that her sister lacks for nothing.

Julia is identical to her great-grandmother Martina, gorgeous with a strong character, a mole by her upper lip, characteristic to the Cabreras, long and jet black hair like her grandmother Julia. The intelligence of her grandfather Erick is evident but so is the bad temper carried in her genes, from her father. It comes from the german ascent of her great-grandfather Roderick Meyer Jr. and the Spanish, from her great-grandmother Martina. Directly, she carries genes of the Mam ethnicity from her father and grandmother Julia. Through her veins runs a unique mix of genes!

In one her trips to the village, she drops the knapsack where she carries her jams and preserves, some of them break and little Victoria is scared, since she know of her sister's horrible temper and only covers her ears so that she can't hear the string of profanities she may say:

—For fuck's sake! These fuckin' pieces of shit are broken for sure!

She keeps on cursing through gritted teeth,

still has not noticed some of them are broken as little Julia stands quietly, aside. Julia stares at her angrily and in a rage continues:

—And you, what the hell are you doin' standing like an idiot?? Move your ass, come help me!

Julia is bent over, picking up what she can of the jams when her eyes see men's boots in front of her and she straightens up immediately. Before she can say a word, the man tells her:

—Such a beautiful woman shouldn't be so angry, much less cuss like that.

Julia places her hands on her waist and wrinkling her forehead, quickly shoots back:

—And who the fuck are you? What in the fucking hell do you care if I'm angry or not or if I cuss however I want?? Don't be nosy!

The handsome young man takes off his hat and with a bow, extends his hand and tells her with a smile:

—Tomás Ambrosio! To serve God and you, lovely irritable one.

She leaves him with his hand extended and the words in his mouth; turns around, pulling Victoria and walks away. Tomás, still laughing, with a mocking voice tells her still:

—I've tamed worse fillies…. This one, won't be an exception!

Julia turns around and makes a rude gesture

with her hand. Victoria, with a friendly smile waves goodbye with one hand.

Tomás hasn't wasted any time since he saw Julia around the market, he's been watching her for weeks but he cannot imagine that she has known from the day he laid eyes on her. Cupid's work is done!

In her saddest, lonely moments, Julia remembers her mother; she stays strong for Victoria, who was only three years old when they became orphans. In Victoria's memories, she has a vague image of her mother and very few memories. The maternal figure in her life has been Julia, who scares her sometimes, so rebellious has she become.

Life has made Julia strong and she remains so; to defend from any danger that may stalk them in the jungle of society and to protect her sister. She did not attend school, not because she didn't want to but rather because she has worked since she was a child and has had to get ahead while also being responsible for Victoria. What little academic formation she has, was taught by her mother. Julia wants her sister to study and asks around the village about the way to accomplish that. Victoria is prepared to start school, Julia bought her everything she needs. When their father learns about it, he forbids it and threatens to lock them inside. That really angers Julia and she wants to leave the house but doesn't know where she could go with her sister, when they are both underage. For the time being she had to desist of the idea of Victoria going to school but she is working on something to help them break free from the yoke of their father.

Every week she takes her jams to the village and starts a new business: buying and selling Mexican products. She has been steadfast due to the promise she made her mother to take care of her little sister. She works hard and earns more money in order to give Victoria a roof and education.

On the first day she had to go buy merchandise she must leave Victoria alone in the big house, this is the first time they are apart. She leaves her under lock and key, with a lot of food, a basin, an oil lamp and a knife to defend herself. She warns Victoria to hide under the bed, in case someone tries to break the door down or if anyone tries to harm her, not to hesitate in using the knife. Julia remembers her mother emphasizing this each time she could. Now she impresses her mother's words on Victoria:

"Regardless of who it may be, nobody has the right to hurt you".

On the way back home, Julia finds Tomás, he is riding a white horse. He offers help to carry the bulk of merchandise she carries on her own head, but she is stubborn as a mule and with her bad temper and plenty of cussing, rejects his help. Upon arriving back at the house, she finds her sister safe and tells her everything that happened, just like their mother did when she told them stories she had experienced.

Victoria is fascinated by Julia's travails. At the house Julia and Victoria try not to run across Chus. After Martina's death the servant made a one-hundred-and-eighty degree turn and more, when she became Demesio's woman. However, Julia ignores her and pays no heed to the insults she receives from the stepmother. She is stronger than ever because that way she can keep Victoria safe. The sisters sleep in the same room and before Victoria goes to sleep, Julia shares the vague memories of the stories their mother used to tell them. Victoria always wants to know and asks yet again

—How was mom?

Julia tells her she tends to look a lot like her mother; these words excite Victoria and she promises Julia she will be just like their mom. Julia says goodnight and with a kiss, retires to her bed. Before going to sleep, Julia braids her hair in two parts. Her hair reaches almost to her ankles since she has never cut it and has remained a virgin. During the day, she braids it to the right side, parted in two and a hair ribbon matching the dress she wears. She's been restless due to an incident that happens at night and is reflected in the morning when she gets up. Hasn't paid any attention to it and for a moment she thinks she is so tired, she's seeing things.

It's been many nights that the same thing happens, she braids her hair in two, every single night. The mystery is figuring out who or what undoes her braids and she wakes up with all her hair combed towards the right side. Tired of the same and thinking perhaps she may be going crazy, she decides to find out what is happening in the middle of the night. She made a mint and ginger infusion to stay awake, only pretending to be asleep.

Past midnight she senses someone at the entrance of the room, slowly opens her eyes and sees a man's silhouette. She notices he wears a huge hat, in the dark, he looks like a cowboy, Tomás' image comes to mind but she thinks:

« But he doesn't wear such a big hat».

As her thoughts distract her, the man is by the side of her bed. She holds tight the knife under the covers but feels her body grow heavy and is unable to move. When the man is in front of her, passes his hands over her braids and she feels like she is suffocating, she remains paralyzed until the next morning. She wakes up and makes her routine chores and then takes Victoria down to the creek, as their mother used to do.

Inside the big house, she searches among her mother's old things and finds some old scissors. She braids her hair and with gritted teeth says

—Let's see if after this you continue bugging me, you son of a hundred thousand whores!

Zas! She cuts half of each braid. That night, before going to bed as usual, she tells stories to her sister until she falls asleep. She drinks her infusion again to stay awake. There's again the man with the big hat, standing by the door. Julia's body starts growing heavy and she loses her breath when the man is by her bed. She feels when the man extends his hand over her braid and, for a moment, everything around her seems frozen. She then hears a moan that makes her shiver and he disappears instantly.

She can hardly sleep in order to stay alert and the next morning, her braids are undisturbed. She refuses to believe the legends and rumors of that region; however, since that day, she gives her story a different turn and she strengthens her spirit even more.

For Julia it wasn't easy to lose her mother at only eight years of age and on top of that be responsible for Victoria. She's taken care of herself and also her sister's wellbeing. That's why she has increased her trips to "the other side" as she calls the border.

The risk is always there every time she crosses the river to seek merchandise. Those are the only days her sister does not join her. She's made it a habit of leaving Victoria under lock and key, believing she is safe until her return. That day their father is drunk beyond measure and enters demanding to know about his eldest daughters and Chus tells him only the younger one is in the room. He comes to the door trying to kick it down, Victoria is scared and does what Julia has told her.

Demesio breaks the door down and comes in looking for the girl. She was under the bed but upon seeing her father, comes out of her hiding place and tells him:

—Oh, daddy, it's you! I got scared thinking it was someone else.

—It's me!

Swaying side to side Demesio comes closer to the girls, lifts her chin with his dirty hand and with his unpleasant alcoholic breath tells her:

—You're looking a lot like your mom...

To which she innocently replies:

—That's what Julia says"

He walks slowly around her, like a wild animal stalking his prey. Suddenly he lifts and throws her on the bed and lands on top of her. Victoria, frightened, screams in desperation and tries to kick out and away from under him.

Suddenly she hears and feels a blow over his old body and with cries Victoria says:

—Little sister! Little sister!!

As she launches herself into Julia.

She carries her and they leave as soon as possible to hide among the bushes. Victoria is still scared and crying and asks Julia not to ever leave her again, to always take her. Julia asks for her forgiveness and tells her she will never leave her again, either and, with sobs, she falls asleep on her sister's chest. To Julia's mind come the memories of the scene told by her mother, how she fell asleep over her granny Chepa's chest. She caresses her head and cries when she thinks about what her own father almost did to Victoria, only ten years old. With sighs, she falls asleep next to her sister. Rain awakes them in the wee hours of the morning. Victoria wakes with a start and Julia hugs and covers her with her own shawl. Tells her they are going back home, not to be afraid, she's there to protect her. Julia comes into the room and still laying there, is her father. She grabs a bucket of water and tosses it over him as that miserable man wakes up not knowing what just happened. Julia reproaches his actions and what he tried to do to Victoria; warns him if he ever touches a hair of her head, she will forget he is their father and is going to rip his genitals and his heart out of his chest. He, still half drunk, on his knees begs her to forgive him.

Tormented by his demons he goes to seek refuge in his own room and never again drinks alcohol but Julia loses all respect for him. She desperately tries to find a place to move to, without success.

Tomás courts her relentlessly, he believes she is old enough to marry without imagining that she is only fifteen. Life made her grow up and mature ahead of her years, she doesn't know since when. That maturity makes her look older than she is. Handsome Tomás sports a few hereditary silver hairs and that male trait makes him seem older, when in reality he is not over twenty yet. He heads for the house and gathers his courage to ask for Julia's hand and respectfully asks Demesio for her in marriage. He's afraid of being rejected by the angry Julia without any idea that she is most interested in getting married. Even though she is in love with him her main objective is giving Victoria a good home.

The wedding takes place in what is left of the house garden. The priest has been brought to Hacienda Martina and they marry with his blessing. Julia has moved to the village and her father doesn't stop her from taking Victoria and they start a new phase in their lives. Just as it happened to the nation, the people begging for a savior from political chaos, the rise in crime and the economy's precipitous fall. They have been granted number five, the Central American Napoleon.

Young Tomás works in another hacienda near the village as a cattleman. He loves his job and together with Julia they build new dreams. Julia has not visited her father since the wedding and hasn't allowed Victoria either. The deep resentment she feels hasn't allowed her to forgive him.

At her sixteen years, Julia is groaning while giving birth to her first son as much as she already knows what it is like to be a mother since she's taken care of Victoria since she was eight years old. Since then, she fears nothing nor anyone.

When he learns his first male grandson was born, her father cannot wait any longer and visits her to meet him. She sees him with anger in her eyes but changes countenance when she sees Demesio's face, sad and overwhelmed. She allows him to see her son, who instantly infuses a new hope of living in Demesio. He is born the day the [27]*monja blanca* is decreed as the national flower of Guatemala. Hard times for most; the press is censored again and the political opposition is executed by firing squad.

Years go by and each one is colored with a

---

[27] Monja blanca: It is a kind of epiphytic orchid

different shade, modesty screams to high heaven and political gags disguise themselves as religious influences.

Advances in infrastructure grow by leaps and bounds. Highways are built with the forced labor of Indians, justified as anti-vagrancy. Progress is as evident as the decline of the people, distant from arts and culture.

Before the light of a new day comes to wake the laggard sleepers of the village, Julia is awake and full of energy. She has a daily routine that she fulfills rigorously and before going on her errands, she cleans every corner of her home. She tells Victoria the first thing to do when she wakes up is to make her bed, and that is the beginning of a good day. With discipline she delivers merchandise at some market stalls, without forgetting her jams and preserves. At the end of each month, Julia tries to keep alive her mother's tradition, recreating a picnic in her huge backyard.

That day she wakes up earlier than usual; there's a full moon and its intense light clears darkness from all angles and she takes advantage of it to sweep her yard. There's a huge mango tree and a few others which provide shade and fruit but also a large amount of trash and dry leaves. Julia sweeps all the leaves gathering them in the center of the yard as she looks for the bag where she places the trash, when she hears a cat's meow.

Looks all around here to see where the meowing is coming from, to no avail. She keeps looking for the sack and suddenly feels a movement in the middle of the trash. She sees a black cat thrashing in the trash and in a matter of seconds it becomes a huge ram. The animal scratches the ground with its rear legs, as if gathering momentum in her direction and takes off running after her. Julia throws the broom and prepares to take the hit. The animal pounces on her placing its front legs on her chest and she, grabbing both of them with all her strength, says:

—You are not going to beat me, fuckin' son of a hundred thousand whores!"

And throws him to the floor, so hard it pirouettes back into the trash. It spins again until it turns back into a harmless cat. With a side glance and meowing runs away from her. Marked by her father's punishment, she is pursued by tormented souls and entities from the afterlife but she is so enormously brave she doesn't fear the devil himself. These supernatural experiences happen constantly but she always faces them with God's help and her own warrior spirit.

Victoria cares for little Catarino, baptized with this name in honor of Katherine, Julia never forgot her great-great-grandmother's name when her own mother Martina mentioned her. She wants to keep her present!

Despite Julia's insistence she could not make Victoria go to school. She knows how to read and write because Julia taught her what little she learned from her mother.

The clock's hands don't stop time and little Catarino steals his grandfather's heart in his short visits. Tomás proposes to Julia letting little Catarino at Demesio's house, one day a week, telling her:

—My beautiful cranky one! That'll be good for both of them.

But he cannot convince her.

He has insisted for a good while until he finally convinces her, when the boy is two years old and easier to care for. Tomás, once a week, leaves the child in Demesio's house on his way to work and picks him up on his way back. Demesio thanks him for the good will in granting him the privilege of seeing his grandson.

Julia feels she is pregnant again and mentions it to Tomás who is thrilled at the news of the arrival of his second child. Events are happening in Julia's favor and soon she is in labor again.

The midwife says:

—It's a boy!

And they call him Tomás like his father.

Victoria has turned into a beautiful young lady, almost identical to her mother; at her fifteen years of age, she falls for a man twenty-five years her senior. Julia doesn't quite approve of this relationship but understands her sister, due to everything they have been through. She gives her approval and blessing.

Only very seldom does Victoria visit Julia since her own wedding. Married life consumes her time not to mention her children.

Catarino grows by his father's side and at a young age rides and tames the wild beasts, still visits his grandfather Demesio every weekend. He's taught him to know the times to sow and harvest, the other gifts he carries in his genes. Catarino loves being with his grandfather and Demesio recovers a measure of reconciliation with the universe. He feels as if life itself granted him a pardon. When Catarino is nine years old he asks his mother to celebrate his grandfather's birthday. It's been eighty-five years that have ran through Demesio's fingers. The celebration is readied in what's left of the big house; Julia makes chicken tamales to celebrate her father. Such harmony flowers between father and daughter that everything seems to radiate happiness. As it happens in the nation, the inauguration of the green palace; a masterpiece which was built with the sweat of prisoners. Every architectural detail precisely selected by the current leader; during the celebration for [28]"el guacamolón" they forget about a movement that begins to display shades of violence. The same happens at the big house; they almost forgot about La Chus, who reappears full of bad energy.

Weeks go by, without turning to look at the leaves left behind by a rainy winter. It marches ahead coloring the streets with brushstrokes of poinsettias, leaving behind the fragrance of newly cut pine trees. The peculiar sound of [29] canchinflines and [30]ametralladoras is a traditional announcement of the arrival of Christmas and a new year. Joyful and full of life, Julia's family gathers together to welcome the start of another year!

Routine continues as usual, according to the pace set by Julia and her life companions.

Catarino asks for permission from his grandfather to celebrate his father's birthday at the big house. Demesio agrees, for he cannot say no to the apple of his eyes and finally feels as if the grandfathers and grandmothers have forgiven him.

---

[28] Guacamolón: Guatemalan slang nickname for the National Palace in the capital city. As it is green in color "guacamolón" simply means a huge guacamole.
[29] Canchinflines: small whistling hand-launched firecracker; whistler.
[30] Ametralladoras: a collection of hundreds of firecrackers strung together.

Julia prepares [31]pepián de chompipe, one of Tomás' favorite dishes. Weather favors the celebration of October 20th and they do so in the backyard of the big house. Almost forgotten in what is considered "the bush" they hear very few of the news from the big city.

The following morning's papers announce a murder: "Lack of respect for life (whoever does not respect one life, does not respect any life)" which took place at La Gloria bridge, one of the triumvirs of the Revolution.

Time marches on to the tic-toc of the clock, without stopping or reversing; same as the evil of men.

Catarino only attended school for a few years, he loves riding next to his father and listening, spellbound, to his grandfather's stories. Julia or Victoria hardly ever visit their father; each one's chores keep them tied to their homes. Despite little Catarino giving back a desire for living to Old Demesio, extending his existence, has been overcome by the years.

La Chus doesn't agree with the close relationship of her husband with his grandson; especially since they talk mostly about the few lands still in his possession. She wanted that time to be dedicated to her own son Victor; however, Victor has learned to overcome blindness and

---

[31] Pepián de chompipe: traditional turkey stew.

learned to see through the eyes of the soul. He has a noble heart and the universe has rewarded him; granted the fortune of meeting young Lucinda, in the middle of puberty he decides to marry her and go live in peace at her hut. Blindly, he learned to mix herbs and by inheritance, makes a living as a healer.

Juana meets a Mexican mule driver and runs away with him; it's known she lives around the shores of Puerto Madero in an orchard of many crops.

Chus' youngest daughter lives in the big house and is courted by an outlaw bent on marrying Maria de Jesús in order to take over her father's land.

Tomás, as is his custom, takes his son to Demesio on weekends. They enjoy those days with many activities. They have stopped hunting due to the fatigue that has overtaken Demesio in the last few years.

On a day when Tomás comes to get Catarino earlier than usual due to the dark clouds announcing the arrival of a serious storm, before coming into the big house, he looks up and thinks he may not have enough time to make it back to the village. He hears voices in the kitchen and slowly gets close to it; stunned for a few seconds, he is shocked by the machinations of Chus and her daughter, also named Chus. He cannot contain his anger and reproaches them; asks what has his little son done for them to wish him dead; they are surprised by his presence and don't know what to say so they start screaming. All the racket attracts the attention of Demesio and little Catarino, who come immediately. Demesio asks what is going on and Tomás only says he's come for his son. The women stay behind, laughing to each other, like hyenas. That same evening, mother and daughter get together with the outlaw. La Chus offers her daughter in exchange of him getting rid of Tomás, together they form a murder plan. Not even a week later and Tomás' body comes up by the shores of river Cabuz; at his thirty-two years of age, his life is stolen by greed and ignorance.

 This is terrible news for Julia, her fairytale life suddenly becomes a nightmare again... now she's alone with two little children. She starts selling many of her household things, money is not enough to pay for rent on her own so she decides to rent a room to tide her over. This adjustment takes her a few years, until Catarino is old enough to do the job his father did.

 He still visits his grandfather not knowing the danger that lurks inside those walls. Little Tomás is shy and lonely, physically very much like his father, he's only seen his grandfather a few times, he's afraid how he looks at him, so he hardly ever visits him. Tomasito, as they call him, spends his time in a carpentry shop near their room, he is focused on learning the craft and dreams of making the best furniture for his mother. At his young age he's an expert of this art and has begun making some furnishings, he's persistent in his plans and whatever he earns he saves in order to have enough capital to set up his own shop.

Catarino is now sixteen years old and just a few days before, together with Tomasito, they plot a surprise for their mother. She rushes from one side to the other of their small room, gathering the ingredients to make a delicious meal for the birthday boy. The fire is burning in the hearth under an open shack at the back of the property and tries to bring everything with her in order not to make multiple trips. She doesn't expect the boys so soon and when they eagerly come into the room, they tell her the food can wait, which annoys her no end since she believes they are suggesting this is a day like any other. Catarino quickly removes her apron and still grumbling they bring her outside. Surprised at their hastiness, she tells them:

—Look, you two knuckleheads! I don't know what you want but at least let me put away my things I have on the hearth and to put the fire out.

Afterwards they take her to the village's exit road to the capital city or the Mexican border. As they get close to their destination, Catarino takes out from his pocket a white handkerchief to blindfold her, which makes her grouchy again even as her sons laugh at her little tantrum, although she agrees to Catarino's desires as she thinks to herself:

«*Remember, Julia, you must be flexible on this special day. But after that... these two will get a lesson!*».

Once they are in front of the house they remove the blindfold and yell in unison:

—Surpriiiseeeee!!!

—What surprise, my ass! Do you want to kill me from a stroke or what the hell??

Catarino, with his romantic charisma tells her:

—A castle for a queen!

Even though he clarifies later on that she deserves much more than that. She is not too convinced and asks what it's all about; Catarino explains they have rented this house for her and they must move as soon as possible, to which she replies, with tears in her eyes:

—What are we going to move if we sold it all?

—Even easier, dear mom, then we move today.

Catarino tells her as he pampers her.

—Now we have room enough to swim in this huge house!

Says Julia wiping her tears.

—Look, mama, I like the house, there's a room for each one of us.

He tells her, without removing his arms from over her shoulders as he points out with his other hand:

—Ah, look! The big open shack there, that's the space for Tomás to get started with his carpentry, without leaving home; look over there... the hearth near the sink and the well, so that my mother doesn't have to get angry because of the old women who steal her stuff and doesn't have to bring water from the neighborhood well or go to the river to do the laundry.

Julia listens intently and think that they have, in fact, realized what she went through in that place but she never complained and remained silent, so as not to worry them. She hears Tomás' voice telling her:

—I've rushed in making the furniture so, dear mom, the house will not be empty.

And they laugh. Moving into their new home, they celebrate Catarino's birthday.

Julia's life finds balance again; she leaves the jams and preserves business and only sells Mexican merchandise now.

Some events have been forgotten, sometimes returning to Julia's memory, as brief sparks of reflection. In the country's urban areas, the idea of democracy stays alive. Quite the opposite from Julia's life, as she'd rather ignore how much she needs some tangible support.

At her door shows up a tall man, greenish eyes, high cheekbones, looking like a [32]gringo.

As she was leaving for the market at that moment, they coincide at the hallway entrance, and she was stunned.

---

[32] Gringo: Guatemalan slang for a white person from the United States.

The handsome man tells her:

—Good afternoon, madam! I'm looking for the carpenter.

She looks him up and down and replies:

—Who's asking?

—Tell him it's the gringo.

She looks him up and down again and gestures in the direction he should go. He goes all the way where Tomás is and when he sees a teenager asks:

—[33]Patojo! I'm looking for your dad.

Tomás is applying varnish and slowly places the brush back in the can and looking up asks:

—Who did you say?

—Your dad.

—Well, look in the cemetery because otherwise, you ain't gonna find him here.

—What do you mean?

Asked the gringo, frowning, confused.

—What you heard, mister. And now please go, I have a lot of work.

Cranky, like his mother.

—They recommended him as the best carpenter in the village, that's why I'm here.

—Well, they lied to you…. I'm the carpenter and I do what I can.

---

[33] Patojo: a young man, the ages between childhood and adulthood.

The man thought he'd find a mature man in this place; he explains what he wants and agrees on a price. He also thinks of the woman he just met, cannot get her out of his head.

Next week, gringo returns for the bed he ordered, likes the work and also requests a dresser. Any excuse to see Julia again.

Gringo just moved to the village, he comes from the cold zone of the territory. He's become good friends with Tomás, after the dresser he wants him to make him another bed. Every now and then he stops by to visit with Tomás who, despite his short age, is a mature young man and gringo likes talking with him. In one of those visits he mentions:

—You know, patojo, I bought some land next to the exit to the cold lands and I'm building myself a little house there.

Tomás lives by the South-central part of the village while Gringo's land is to the North. Tomás asks:

—How come you're here on the coast, far from your native place?

He summarizes his story. Had a bad fight with his older brother over their father's land. The father wanted to split the land between the two of them and give them their inheritance while still alive. The older brother lusts after all the land and gringo, in order not to cause his mother any pain over seeing them fight, decided to leave. He tells him he sells coffee in his free time; in addition to "Gringo" he's also known as "the coffee baron". Tomás, with curiosity, asks what he does when is not in his "free time", he replies he is a military commissioner. His Gringo nickname was earned because he always says a few words in English.

Catarino still frequents his grandfather, who's still standing despite his age. Things calm down with La Chus, whose daughter ends up shacking up with the outlaw, under her orders.

Three years have passed, which Gringo uses courting Julia. Her sons agree to the relationship, except her. With Tomás prodding, widow Julia marries El Gringo Arturo Barrios. Julia still lives with her sons, she hasn't moved to Gringo's house, it's like they never married. Julia is already pregnant a few months later and hasn't said anything to her husband, nobody knows, her belly unnoticeable. Catarino has suffered two murder attempts, neither one of which was successful, he is very effective at defending himself with the machete, a skill learned from his grandfather, and a good rider, just like his father. Despite the danger, he won't stop visiting his grandfather. Demesio is an elderly man and all he wants is to leave his land to his grandson as a legitimate inheritance. Julia's sons are making their own way in life.

Catarino meets a good looking woman, most men fight over her but not one will be responsible for getting her out of that life. Catarino takes her out of prostitution. He never frequented those places so no one understands why he brings her home, particularly when he is already in a relationship with a young lady from a fine family, whom he ends up leaving for her. Julia knows something is wrong in that relationship, the woman behaves well enough but there's something which doesn't convince Julia. She starts her own investigations and wants to know why her son is so crazy about her. The woman treats him well, cares for him and one way or another is slowly earning Julia's affection but her sixth sense won't let her be. By chance she notices the empty jar for the [34]frescos, gets curious and goes to find her daughter-in-law in the room, she has her back turned to her and doesn't notice Julia's presence. She only observes and before her son arrives, she waits for him at the corner of the block.

Catarino is surprised by his mother standing there, dismounts the horse and says:

—Mommy, what are you doing here, did something happen?

—No, [35]mijo, I discovered something I

---

[34] Fresco: a sweet, cool beverage usually drunk at lunch time.
[35] Mijo: Guatemalan slang for "my son" a contraction of the Spanish "mi hijo"

disliked, I knew there was something about that little woman of yours!

Catarino, somewhat miffed about the way his mother talks about his woman, says:

—Come on, mom! She's good, I don't like for you to see her as bad.

Julia places her hands on her hips and says with an angry voice:

—Well, it's your problem if you want to be a [36]pendejo! I saw her washing her own [37]pushaca and make your fresco with that water; word to the wise, it's not that I see her as bad, I just don't like what she does to you.

And walks away. When he comes into the house, the woman greets him like every day, food served and a big jar of fresco on the table. Catarino is running his mother's words in his head; the woman sits down, as she does every day, to watch him eat. When she serves his drink, he asks her to drink it herself. Surprised, she insists she's already eaten; he insists she drinks from the beverage in the jar. She cannot believe she's been found out and pretends to be offended.

Catarino is enraged and throws everything off the table; she locks herself in the room. For many days Catarino doesn't sleep with Carlota,

---

[36] Pendejo: an insult widely used throughout Latin America. Stupid, "dumbass"

[37] Pushaca: Vagina

she becomes depressed but that doesn't make him return to her. No one knows when she left the house and the village and was never heard from again.

Tomás falls in love with a young lady from a wealthy family, she wants him to court her but he keeps thinking:

«*I'm a simple carpenter*».

And due to his own insecurity, makes things difficult for the relationship.

Julia gathers her husband and sons and announces she is pregnant, the news is a cause for great joy. She has everything ready for the delivery.

MIGRANT DESTINY

FIFTH GENERATION

Three days after the celebration of Independence Day, the midwife is attending to Julia, it rains harder than usual in the place. Tomás is desperate and under the torrential rain goes looking for Gringo while Catarino goes for his grandfather in order to have his blessing for the new joy of the family. Arturo hopes for his first boy, the midwife yells:
—"It's a girl!
Arturo is very moved, despite not having a boy and cries when he has his little girl in his arms. In the meantime, national events do not stand still, there is rumor of a counter-revolution.
Arturo registers his little one as Violeta. Despite her birth, Julia refuses to go live with Arturo, remaining in the rented house. Catarino adores his little sister, taking her with him when he goes to visit his grandfather, riding on the horse in front of him. She loves joining her brother.

Julia still comes and goes to "the other side", as they call crossing the border. Julia notices something unusual in her menstrual cycle and bleeds irregularly but pays no attention and believes she is just tired. She misses her period the next three months but it returns on the fourth. Now she is worried and goes to visit the midwife. She tells her she is pregnant again and to be very careful, for it looks like a risky pregnancy, she needs a lot of rest.

Julia gathers her family again and shares the news, without mentioning the midwife's warning so as not to worry them. She decides to rest on her own. Although the boys know the reason, they find it strange to see her inactive, especially since it didn't happen that way when she expected Violeta.

On Friday, the day Catarino usually visits his grandfather, he rises earlier than usual. Julia already lit the fire to make coffee.

—Good morning, mommy! What are you doing up so early?

—Good morning, mijo! I feel a little restless, is all. Coffee will be ready soon, let me get the girl.

—No, mom, she's not coming with me today, I'm going to be late and I don't want to have her with me too late tonight.

Catarino doesn't take his sister Violeta that

day and Julia says goodbye like she never has before. A few minutes after Catarino left, her water breaks ahead of schedule. Tomás wakes up due to her screams, runs for the midwife and also his stepfather. The delivery wasn't complicated, she was just premature at seven months. The mother's health has been very good, which helped the birth and despite being born early, the baby is healthy, a little small. So much so she fits in a shoe box.

Catarino is with his grandfather, who takes him into the cave. Demesio goes there every now and then, only by special request as he's almost finished, nearing a century of life. They talk in the cave for a long time, it's almost night. Demesio asks Catarino to stay with him, as a foreboding sticks in his throat. Catarino tells him he cannot stay, even though his mother never said a word, he knows something's not right with her pregnancy and thinks it's a delicate situation, which is why he wants to be near her. He hugs his grandfather so tightly, as if it were a permanent farewell and gets his blessing, as he always does when they say goodbye; except on this occasion with teary eyes. As if he were holding on for dear life, the old man doesn't want to let go of his grandson. The Chuses laugh mockingly, like hyenas.

Demesio heads for his room and lights a few candles. Catarino mounts his horse and heads for the village at a quick trot; almost one kilometer from the entrance to the village, he's ambushed. At the very same time a soldier murders the president of the nation, Catarino falls to the ground from a shot that drops him from the horse. They shoot him many times, without hitting once, sicarios passing for revolutionaries. They surround him and he defends himself with his only protection, his machete. He wounds many but it's not enough, they have shot him point-blank. Some peasants hear the shooting and fire their lamps looking for the direction whence they come. That alerts the murderers who, before leaving the scene, go to Catarino and tell him he should have distanced himself from Demesio when his father died and concludes saying:

—This is an order from Chus.

As he sliced his throat with his knife. They mount their horses and disappear in the middle of the night. A blowing wind snuffs out Demesio's candles and he rises from his bed with a horrible chill which makes him cry.

Catarino's horse carried on home, alone, when he fell from him. Julia hears the horse neigh and when she sees him alone, doesn't care she just delivered a baby and gets on her son's horse. He takes her back to where Catarino is, surrounded by people bearing torches. He's still alive, holding his own neck in order not to bleed out and when he sees his mother riding the horse, breaks out crying. Julia gets off the horse at once and sees her son laying on the ground, all bloody. She cries trying to break through the crowd. Catarino is choking in his own blood, almost unable to speak, holds his mother's hand, draws Julia closer and gargles:

—La Chus!

Kisses his mother and his strength fades, let's her hand go, fully bleeding out. Julia screams with all her strength and hugs him tightly. Julia appears mad, the agitation of her body is beyond her strength. Someone draws close and puts his hand on her shoulder and tells her:

—I saw them, Doña Julita! Calm down! There'll be time for revenge.

They bring Catarino to the village and Julia vows to avenge her son's death. She buries him in the village cemetery, next to his father.

Due to Julia's carelessness when riding the horse the same day she delivered a child, has been admitted to the departmental hospital. She got irreversible damage to her reproductive system, requiring emergency surgery which leaves her empty inside. The baby, baptized as Margarita by her father Arturo, is also hospitalized with her mother, both under observation for a month.

When Julia leaves the hospital, she starts to investigate those that murdered her son. She has located them.

Two months later, the evening of October 20th, there's widespread protests over voting in the elections and Julia learns her father is gravely ill and wishes to see her daughters. Julia grabs her sister, Victoria and together they head for the big house, around nine in the evening. Distance seems to grow longer on foot, four to five hours. The road is silent except for the loud chirping of crickets and a starry sky. They're almost to the river, which marks the distance left to the big house. The old parish clock strikes midnight. Julia senses they're being followed and grasps a knife in the pocket of her dress even as she feels her body growing heavier. Victoria turns to look and scared, tells her sister she thinks she sees a man with a big hat, riding a black bull. Julia doesn't stop and on the contrary, tries to speed up telling her sister to do the same. As they walk she removes a rosary from her neck and places it on Victoria, telling her to remove her clothes as she walks and to put them on inside out. Julia is also doing this and takes out a long tie from the knapsack she always carries for her purchases. She ties it around Victoria's waist to her own and tells her, no matter what, not to open her eyes and to keep walking by her side. Julia makes a cross with her long braid and with hasty steps keeps on praying until they get to the shoreline. They hear the bull bellow behind them. Suddenly, out of the blue, it starts raining hard, as if to clear evil spirits from their way. Julia also takes out a couple of ocotes and places them on the floor in the **shape of a cross.** She tells Victoria they are going to cross the river and it must be as quick as possible because the river is rising and turbulent, the current will grow strong and they won't be able to cross. The water doesn't reach higher than their waists, they're about to make it to the other shore when suddenly the current grabs Victoria. Making a great effort Julia pulls Victoria out and drags her to shore. Good thing they were tied together, otherwise the current would have taken her away. On the other side, only the silhouette of the man riding the bull can be seen. They continue on their way and Julia leaves crosses with the kindling sticks. Demesio is a couple of months away from being a century old but his sadness over the death of his grandson was so great, he wouldn't even leave his bed. When he sees his daughters arrive, he begs their forgiveness again, gives them his blessing and asks to be buried next to Martina. With a peaceful sigh, his hands intertwined with his daughters'… he leaves this world. Demesio didn't have time to finish off his grandson's murderers but he did take out the intellectual author of it. Days later, La Chus becomes ill with pneumonia and starts vomiting blood, an agonizing punishment which didn't last long enough.

A year after her son's death, Julia has located the murderers. One by one, they've been eliminated and she ripped out her outlaw brother-in-law's heart with her own hands. Crime must be punished so that the world remains in balance and souls can rest in peace. When she's about to do the same with her half-sister, her son's soul floating around her tells her he has been avenged. Maria de Jesús begs for mercy and forgiveness for her mother's and husband's actions. Julia is blinded by her pain but lets her go and never sees her again.

Her mother, La Chus, over the last few days of Demesio's life, when he was bedridden, was able to grab his hand and place his fingerprint on some papers, leaving her daughter Maria de Jesús as the only heir of the land that's left.

Maria de Jesús doesn't know what to do with so many tragedies and finds refuge in alcohol, selling land and in a short time, nothing is left. All she has is a piece of land where she builds a hut. The big house has been demolished by its new owners.

Julia's life was marked by her son's death. She cannot find peace in the midst of such sadness. Tomás pampers her, trying to get her attention. One day, seeing her turned into an ice floe, takes her in his arms and reminds her that Catarino wasn't her only son, there's him and his sisters, who also need her. She reacts and starts paying a bit more attention to her remaining children.

Tomás stops courting Rosario, despite both being in love. Her parents have arranged a marriage for her with a local wealthy young man. Tomás has no vices but when he learns this news, goes into one of the new bars popping up in the village and gets so drunk he passes out. He's not used to visiting such places, much less after what happened to his brother. He loses his head and ends up waking up in a prostitute's bed. He pays her, apologizes and leaves, without giving it much importance. He seeks refuge in his work in order to forget Rosario, who he never seeks again after receiving the news of her engagement.

Julia seldom goes for merchandise across the border, it's not as safe as it used to be. It's very risky now due to the conflict between the two countries and the death of some Mexican fishermen. It's now popular to refer to the merchandise from Mexico as "smuggling". Whatever one can buy is taken across the dividing river, hidden even in one's underwear so that it's not found by customs officers.

Christmas came and went in a flash. Julia doesn't much care about the season, but that

December thirty-first she arose at dawn to follow the tradition learned from her mother. Martina made the best tamales in the region from a recipe learned from her granny Chepa.

Since then, Julia makes tamales on December thirty-first. She recalls her mother telling her December twenty-fourth wasn't as important as the thirty-first, a new beginning for everything, she used to say. Since very early she's focused on the preparations and lost in her memories of that day, when she's surprised out of her reverie by a distant howling; knowing the tormented souls from the afterlife never leave her alone, heads in that direction with a handful of salt, for throwing it to whatever is howling… since that time she had to chase a cat which cried like a baby. Walking towards the door, where the crying is coming from, when she opens it and finds a newborn, crying loudly. Those cries awake Tomás, who comes to the door, half-asleep. He scratches his head when he sees his mother with the baby, she explains what happened and places it on the table. In front of Tomás' eyes she unwraps it, to know its gender.

—It 's a boy!

Says Julia. Before she could say another word, she is silenced by a note stuck to the baby's belly, addressed to Tomás:

Dear Tomás:

The night we slept together, I became pregnant, I didn't say anything since then.
I can't keep the baby, you keep him, he's your son.
You'll never hear from me again, never tell him who his mother is, you can tell him I died at childbirth.
The Whore.

Tomás' eyes open wide as he reads and they are both stunned at this news. Julia tells him her husband and she will adopt the baby and give him their name. Tomás thanks her good intentions but tells her he will take on his responsibility. To honor his dead brother, he names the baby Catarino. A big blessing to start a new year.

Julia's daughters start school but stop after elementary.

Time keeps on running and the country has seen little progress. Violence has risen and common crime is out of control; with murder rampant, the elderly lament "if only we had [38] Ubico!" yearning for the strongman credited with eliminating crime and delinquency.

Violeta is courted by a nice young man, tall and skinny; with long, curly blond hair and eyes green like the jungle, his greatest defect fault

---

[38] Ubico: General Jorge Ubico (1878 – 1946), dictator credited with reducing crime and delinquency during his mandate.

being a shameless scoundrel. Even though he is married with two daughters he still chases Violeta. She rejects all his attempts, many times she has told him so. She's warned him that, unless he stops bothering her, she will tell her brother, he's just so insistent. He is not, of course, Violeta's only pretender, her appeal was inherited from her grandmother, Martina, she shines anywhere she goes.

Walking the streets of that colorful village, there is a very handsome young man, in a police uniform, who won't wait any longer and comes to Tomás' shop to tell him of his good intentions towards his sister. Violeta is not interested in anyone at all. She has different plans for her life, works in a clothing store and saves every penny she earns to travel to the capital city, her dream is to be a fashion designer and get far away from her bothersome sister.

She's seventeen years old and has enough money saved for her trip. She's happy because she will make her dreams come true, it's her last days of work and she already announced her departure to the store's owners, who express their regret at losing such a wonderful worker. That morning, she's running late and takes a taxi in order to be on time. She rushes into the back seat without noticing who is driving the car. She realizes it's the man who's been after her all this time.

—Good morning, beautiful! Where to?

Says the cab driver with an intimidating smile.

—Oh, it's you.

Violeta says, none too thrilled and asks:

—To the store, please.

Without looking at him, she searches her purse for the money to pay for the ride and when she looks up she realizes they're going in another direction. She warns the driver and tells him he missed her destination. He laughs out loud and tells her today is his day off and they will have a good time. Violeta starts screaming, asking him to go back as she reminds him that if she took a cab, the reason was her being very late. He completely ignores her words and keeps on driving. Violeta, in desperation, starts hitting him from behind and he stops the car behind some bushes. Exits the car and opens the rear door and without wasting time, pounces on Violeta. She screams for him to get off her and to take her to work. He tells her he's never been rejected by a woman as he rips off her underwear. She kicks without success and in a matter of seconds, he has raped her. She is so ashamed and humiliated at having her innocence violated and is paralyzed inside the car. Scared and shaking impotently, cries disconsolately. A coward, he only laughs mockingly. He drops her off in front of her job, she is so ashamed she cannot even go in, hugging herself and head hanging low she tries to hide from what people might think, walks in the direction of her house. No one notices her and she tears an old blouse into strips and dips them in alcohol. Carefully she wipes her private parts, she wants to disinfect the abuse off her and also wipes her face, not wanting to look haggard. After cleaning herself, she places the strips in her purse to be thrown away, far from her house. She prepares a small suitcase with her important things, takes her savings out of its hiding place and writes a farewell note:

Mom, Dad, Brother:
Don't worry about me, I leave for the city, I'm going to work and study what I like. I love you so much.
Violeta.

She doesn't mention her sister Margarita as they never got along since they were little. They fight over everything and have a deathly rivalry. Margarita is jealous of Violeta due to the attention she gets from her father and brother. The few photographs that their mother had of them, she damaged… cannot even look at each other in a picture. After Violeta's departure, the house is sad and cold, Margarita still doesn't get the same attention as her sister did, which fills her with even more resentment.

The rapist, Neftali, is worried because he hasn't seen Violeta since that very sad day (for her). He's asked around but no one tells him anything, it's like the Earth swallowed her.

Margarita begins work at the same store where her sister did; she's courted by the owner's son and she likes him. One day, Julia brings lunch to her at the store and when going inside she runs into a businessman who delivers merchandise to the store.

—Watch where you're going, moron!

Julia tells the man.

He apologizes and leaves.

Margarita is surprised at her mother's visit and tells her she's about to go eat lunch. She thanks her mother for the kind gesture of bringing lunch to her, they talk for a bit and they discuss the man that almost ran her over at the entrance. Margarita explains he is a local businessman delivering merchandise.

Meanwhile, in the city, Violeta finds a job caring for an elderly woman. She's provided a room to live there, since the lady's grown sons are painters and they travel throughout Europe exhibiting their work. Violeta likes the job, despite it not being her life's dream, she dedicates plenty of time and attention to the lady since a different servant performs other chores.

Violeta gets worried when she misses her period for two straight months. She asks for permission to have a Monday off, which the lady approves but is now suspicious. Violeta goes to a medical clinic to be examined and after a while, the nurse comes out smiling and tells her:
—Congratulations! You're pregnant!
She leaves, devastated and with teary eyes, walks all the way to the house where she works, trying to clear her mind. When she arrives, the lady asks her:
—Violeta, what's the matter?
She tells her what is happening. She waits for the sons to return from their last trip and quits the job, her belly now showing.
Eight months pregnant Violeta returns home. As she gets off the bus, she runs into her old pretender, the policeman. He, surprised at her pregnancy, asks whether she got married. While she waits for her luggage, Violeta replies in the negative. Lies to him saying it was a one-night stand in the city. He continues interrogating her and asks if her family knows. She shakes her head, answering no, while he offers his support, telling her they can say he got her pregnant and will take responsibility by marrying her. Violeta thanks him for his gesture but says she will face her misfortune alone. He walks her to the door, helping with the luggage she carries. Tomás sees

the policeman but doesn't recognize his sister until she's inside. Tomás drops the saw he's using to cut a board and responding to the noise, Julia comes out. They question her, severely, and tell her she's not welcome there for being a shameless hussy. Without saying a word, she goes to her room and cries until the next day.

Julia and Arturo still live separately, something Julia decided since they were married.

The next day, Violeta goes to visit her father and asks to stay at his house. He doesn't question her about what happened, tells her his house is her house and he's just happy she is back. The house is mostly bare, the only furniture, those that Tomás made years ago. They are not needed by Arturo since he hardly ever stays there, always traveling for his coffee business.

Tomás looks for the policeman without success. He assumes he is responsible for dishonoring his sister. Despite his anger over these events he is excited about becoming an uncle and while he figures what to do with his sister's situation, he builds her a little cradle. Before Violeta gives birth, Tomás visits her. Taking her by the arms he insists she tell him the truth. Yelling, he asks:

—Is the policeman the father of the child you expect?

He shakes her so much, finally she screams:

—YES!! And leave me alone, I will raise my baby!

Tomás looks for the cop for many days; in the middle of the village fair celebration, on his day off, the policeman is enjoying himself in a cantina. He's drinking with another cop when Tomás enters and challenges him. The policeman, already drunk, tells Tomás:

—I didn't make your whore of a sister pregnant!

Tomás goes berserk and takes the gun he had in his belt and shoots him twice. The other cop tries to take out his own gun but Tomás is quicker and shoots him, too. Everybody runs out screaming while the bodies of both policemen lie in a pool of blood. Tomás is frozen with anger and once he reacts, he runs out of the place and heads home. When Julia sees him looking pale, she asks:

—Mijo, what's the matter? You look like you're running away from death, you're white as a sheet of paper!

Tomás tells her what just happened and she immediately takes him to her sister Victoria's house. Tells him to wait there while she looks for some things at home. The police are already looking for Tomás in every corner of the village. As is usual in the small towns of the countryside, rumors fly and suddenly they say he is a guerrillero. Earlier that same year the [39]EGP was

Police arrive at Julia's house, looking for Tomás and Julia tells them she hasn't seen him.

—Why are you looking for him?

She asks to divert their attention. They give her the answer she already knows. Well into the night of December 10th, Julia takes Tomás across the border. She knows those crossings back and forth and she takes him across the river, boarding a bus to Tuxtla Gutierrez, in Mexico, and leaves him in a room. She also leaves clothes and money enough for about a year while she promises to return within that period or until things calm down. Police come the next day to visit Violeta and when she learns what happened, runs to her mother's house but finds no one there. She then heads to her best friend's house, they talk about the events and her friend tells her to calm down, for the baby's sake. When her friend sees Violeta so upset over those events, she offers her a glass of sugared water but before she can drink even a sip, she feels herself wet. The stress and restiveness of the last few days have caused her water to break. Violeta asks her friend Elena to please bring the midwife to her father's house and to meet her there, she will go ahead now.

---

[39] EGP: "Ejército Guerrillero de los Pobres" or Guerrilla Army of the Poor, a Guatemalan leftist guerrilla movement.

MIGRANT DESTINY

SIXTH GENERATION

Violeta arrives home, holding her belly and as she opens the door, her contractions begin. She lays on top of a [40]petate and begins pushing and groaning. The birth came days early due to her aggravation at her brother added to the strong impression she received when she learned of the murders. Desperate at being alone she pulls a bed sheet and covers herself. Moaning and groaning in the midst of that empty house, screaming out of pain, she feels a huge relief when she hears a baby cry. She knows she is fine due to the constant wails of the baby, echoing around the house. She passes out from fatigue. After a few moments, Arturo comes in, calling out:

—[41]Mija! I'm home early!

Only the baby's cry is heard. He enters Violeta's room and sees his daughter, looking as if she's dead. He screams in fright at the same time as Elena arrives with the midwife.

---
[40] Petate: small mat made of dried palm leaf.
[41] Mija: Feminine form of "mijo", short for "mi hija"

The midwife asks for hot water and clean rags. Arturo goes to the hearth to light the fire and boil the water. The midwife places some alcohol under Violeta's nose to make her come to. The she announces:

—It's a girl! She looks like an angel.

She wraps her in a white blanket and hands her over to Arturo. He cries seeing his granddaughter although he wanted a boy. They comfort Violeta in bed and give her daughter to her arms. She cries when she sees her, identical to her own father. No one knows who that baby's father is. Arturo celebrates unholstering his pistol and firing shots into the air. There's also a celebration in the capital city due to the fifth anniversary of the Nobel prize for literature.

Violeta tries to feed her daughter, who is very hungry but as soon as she tries a few drops of her mother's milk she vomits it back. The midwife tells her:

—Maybe your milk is no good.

To which Elena asks:

—How can you say that, lady?

The midwife insists some women have bad milk and that it's poison for their newborn babies. She points out to Elena a welt the baby developed where she got a drop of milk. Elena goes looking for a doctor friend of hers so that he can check out her friend and her baby.

The doctor checks Violeta and upon learning she had her child alone, tells her she is a strong young woman and doesn't appear to have any complications. About the baby, on the surface, presents a delicate prognosis. The doctor emphasizes it, saying:

—I have to do some blood tests in order to know exactly why she doesn't tolerate her mother's milk. In the meantime, feed her boiled water with a little sugar"

She was just born and is already suffering the syringe's prick. Her life has already been lived crying in hunger and Violeta cannot console her.

—Let me have her!

Says Arturo holding the baby, who immediately calms down, having developed a close connection with her grandfather. The doctor indicates he will take the samples to the laboratory, himself, and hopes to have them as soon as possible.

Margarita returns home devastated as the news of what happened to her brother has spread like wildfire. People who did not see the incident find it hard to believe what Tomás is accused of. They insist he is a good man. Margarita comes to Arturo's house looking for her mother only to find out her sister has given birth. She lunges at her sister, not caring she just delivered a baby, and shakes her and yells:

—It's your fault these things are happening to the family!

Arturo pulls her off by her arms and orders her to leave. He cannot believe Margarita would treat her sister in such a way, after she just had a baby... as if she were her worst enemy. Margarita returns home, so ashamed over everything she keeps hearing about her family, she didn't even go to work. There she waits for her mother's return.

The doctor returns with the test's result the week after the baby's birth and tells her she has a genetic disease, an incompatible blood type. She suffers hereditary spherocytosis; Violeta asks him to speak plainly, so he answers she will have anemia her whole life. He gives her a prescription for a specific type of milk, not really convinced it will have good results. He sends Gringo to buy the milk. When he returns Violeta asks for the milk and he replies with a shocked expression:

—That milk is expensive as gold! What you gave me wasn't even enough for a single ounce and I didn't have any more money on me.

—Oh, my god, dad! How much is it? I thought I was giving you enough money for two big cans.

—One can costs what five large cans of [42] Nido costs!

---

[42] Nido: "Leche Nido" the most common powdered milk for infants in the Guatemalan market at the time.

Violeta is stunned at the cost of the milk for her daughter. Arturo returns to the pharmacy for the special milk and prepares the bottle, just as the doctor indicated. She was only able to hold it down for a couple of hours. The strong reaction gives the baby diarrhea and not knowing what to do, they race to the doctor again. He tells them, maybe the only milk good for her, and there's no guarantee, is only sold in "the other side" (Mexico) and if they thought the first one was expensive... this is one much more so.

—This little girl is so delicate! Seems like the stork made a mistake in delivery!

Says Arturo laughing.

—Ay, dad! You may be right... yeah, she doesn't even have the Mongolian spot.

And they laugh just so that they won't cry. The little baby starts crying, as if she understands they're talking about her. Not even imagining she has the blood of different races and gifts. Violeta is anguished, seeing that almost all her savings go towards a single can of milk, that her father had to go find across the border. Just as the doctor predicted, this is the only milk that the baby can tolerate.

After a few days, Julia returns after Margarita tells her Violeta had her baby already. She feels such rage against her own daughter, believing it's her fault that her son ruined his life for her. She heads to her husband's house, yelling and cursing the tragedy afflicting her family, her hand raised to slap Violeta. Arturo has the baby in arms but is still able to hold her hand and tells her to calm down. Julia howls like a wounded animal in pain when Arturo tells her:

—Look, Julia, your granddaughter! Look at the most beautiful thing life has given us! Just look!

Julia stops and like a miracle, the baby smiles at her and Julia cannot help herself and starts crying. As if pulled by a strange magic, she gets close and holds the baby, holding on tight so that she heals her pain from before. After this, Julia starts moving her things to Arturo's house. She places Tomás' tools in a wooden case and plans to take them to him when she next goes to visit. After one month, Margarita and Catarino have also moved to Gringo's house. Then they get an unexpected visit from the finance ministry; Arturo hasn't paid taxes on his properties for many years and all his lands are confiscated, except his house. Violeta tried to pay off this debt but it was too late, the land was auctioned off to the wealthy people in the village.

Violeta has run out of money for her daughter's milk and decides to return to the capital city to work. She knows what life is like there and that she can make a lot more money there instead of just staying in the village. Her dream of becoming a fashion designer has been replaced with the dream of seeing her daughter healthy. She says goodbye to the little two-month old baby with her blessing and promises she will soon return for her.

Violeta seeks out the painter sons of the lady she used to care for, hoping and praying they would still remember her. They have not been able to find anyone better to replace her and the old lady hugs her when she sees her and asks about her pregnancy. Violeta updates her on what's happened to her.

Julia holds on to her granddaughter as if she's her guardian angel against the demons that accost her. Margarita warms up to her also and for Catarino, she is a little porcelain doll; of course, she is the apple of her grandfather's eyes.

Arturo had her registered as Martina Lucia Barrios. "Martina" for her great-grandmother and Lucia for the village's patron saint, with her mother's last name.

Gringo works hard in his coffee business and is joined by Catarino, who is fascinated with his grandfather's company, whom he has loved and respected as far back as he can recall. Margarita goes to work in the village's community pharmacy and Julia continues her own business while still caring for her granddaughter. She searches for a nanny to help her take care of her.

Their simple little wooden house with a tin roof, with long hallways... is full of joy with the cries and laughter of the little one. They made a room for Martina Lucia and Julia ordered they finish her cedar crib, which Tomás had started building.

Every time Julia goes for milk across the border, brings little things here and there for the little girl, on one of those occasions she purchases a peach-colored mosquito net so that her granddaughter is not bitten... since there are many in that area. Martina grows up healthy and with fine genes. Her grandfather also designed a coffee dryer so that she can play while he works.

She's both delicate and curious, crawling from one side to the other of that large wooden coffee dryer. She observes closely the surrounding grounds but doesn't dare touch it. Eventually, curiosity wins and she grabs a handful of dirt. When she sees her dirty hand, she starts screaming, bringing everyone's activities to a halt and to run to her, scared, expecting the worst. They think maybe she's been bitten by some animal. She shows her hand showing the dirt on it and her grandmother wipes it clean with a moist rag. She watches her own hand closely, realizing it's now clean. She smiles at her grandmother and stays quiet.

Julia tells her:

.—You can't speak but girl, you make yourself understood! With that big smile, you can steal everybody's heart. You're not even one year old and you're very smart. Thank God!

Martina Lucia listens to her grandmother intently and babbles "ma ma" a couple of times. Julia melts with emotion before her granddaughter's first words. From that day on, Martina Lucia never again touched the dirt.

The nanny doesn't know how to tell Julia that she cannot continue working for her. She is engaged and will soon get married. Her future husband is taking her to another village. She finally speaks with Julia and indicates she has to leave her job but recommends another young woman who really needs to work. Julia understands her reasons and asks to see the other girl.

She meets with the new girl and indicates how much in need of her services she is and asks whether she can start work immediately. The girls says yes and starts working the same day; Julia shares the basic instructions and important facts about the baby, telling her:

—She is a girl who won't bother you, cries only when she is wet and screams louder if she's pooped; cries when she is hungry, cries if her hands or her clothes are dirty, cries when she is sleepy. If she's clean, has eaten and got sleep and still cries, something else is wrong, but normally those are the only reasons.

Julia walks around the kitchen showing the girl where to find each thing she may need, everything is in order and continues:

—Her clothes are washed with camay soap and then we boil it. The pink string outside is for the baby's clothes only and the water for her bottle is in that green thermos

Pointing at the area where only the baby's things are kept. She inhales and continues again:

—As you can see, all her stuff is there, please find everything as you found it, I don't like having a mess.

As she shares these instructions Julia looks for the sacks for the market and finishes by saying:

—For now just watch her while I go to the market; she's eaten and clean and just had her nap.

The new nanny only says:

—Oh, of course Doña Julita! Don't worry, I'll take care of her" even as she thinks to herself:

«Ummm! What is she, the "princess of Spain"?? Ummm, you may be cute, little [43]*ishta but if she thinks I'm going to be her servant... she's crazy!»

Julia is only one block away when she

---

[43] Ishta: young girl

realizes she forgot her wallet and turns around to return to the house. As she goes in she hears the baby crying, runs into the house and cannot believe her own eyes! The new "nanny" is beating the baby with a carnation stalk.

Julia feels like she wants to die when she sees her granddaughter with marks on her legs from the perverse whipping she just got. She grabs her hand and starts also whipping her with the same stick. Sobbing, the nanny tells her the baby started crying for no reason, she wouldn't shut up and exhausted her patience. Julia orders her to disappear before she does something crazy. She holds the baby asking for her forgiveness, for leaving her with a stranger. Martina won't stop sighing, she falls asleep but suddenly jumps, scared, and starts crying again. She runs a fever and Julia grabs a red kerchief, she counts exactly twenty-seven pepper seeds, garlic, chile and an egg. Ties everything inside the kerchief and passes it all over the girl's little body and places the bundle under her shirt. Not before long the baby falls asleep again, sighing. After a good while Julia burns the bundle, places it among the embers in the hearth and moves it around, it making it look like fireworks, as she says:

—May your eyes and hands burn for the damage you did to my granddaughter!

Repeating other hard-to-understand

incantations through gritted teeth. This calms the baby down as her fever cools down.

A few days later she finds a good girl, who cares for the baby as if she were a porcelain doll, with evident love.

Julia dresses Martina with a lacy yellow dress and white shoes with a jingle bell in front. It's her christening day and the first picture of her life. Magdalena and her husband Humberto ask to be her godparents, a young, just married couple from families of renown in the village, as a show of charity, as many wealthy people used to do, forgetting the children immediately after the ceremony.

Violeta never stopped sending money to Julia for her daughter's support and in one of her telegrams she asks her mother to travel to the capital city and bring the baby with her. So Julia comes to visit her daughter one year after she left and while Violeta hugs and kisses her child, the girl cries and squirms since her own mother is a stranger to her. The elderly lady whom Violeta cares for tells her they don't need to go to a hotel, her family can stay with her in the house, in her own room or any other, they have more than enough space. The baby conquered everyone's hearts in that house. They didn't stay long, just for the weekend.

At the end of every year, Julia brings Martina

Lucia to visit her mom, leaves her for three weeks and then comes back for her. During that period of time, Julia goes to visit her son, nobody knows where he is. He makes himself a new life and with his talent for carpentry, soon he is the owner of his own shop.

Violeta buys toys to keep her little one entertained but she has no interest in them; what she likes is books. So Violeta starts buying her notebooks and crayons, teaching her to read and write. Violeta saddens every time Julia comes to get the girl but she cannot keep her by her side full time. The lady of the house is in very delicate health and she must attend to her almost twenty four hours a day. That prevents her from tending to her daughter. The painters are also sad because their mother is now seriously ill, reason for which she is visited by many artists, who come to offer their support. A friend they haven't seen in a long time visits them, Marco Castro, a sculptor. Having taken a seat in the living room, Violeta comes bearing a tea tray. Interrupting their conversation:

—Good evening! If I may… the maid has taken a few days off and I'd be glad to serve you.

The painters thank Violeta for her gesture. The sculptor is stunned by her beauty and immediately asks:

—Who is she?

The younger of the brothers, the most arrogant one, disparagingly says:

—She's just a country bumpkin!

To which Marco replies with mischievous smile and a deep "radio voice":

—Well, what a lovely "country bumpkin" and what a bearing!

The older brother laughs out loud and says:

—Well, we're not blind either.

Both brothers have hidden their sexual preferences to avoid prejudice although their manners would give them away to someone who knows.

After serving the gentlemen, Violeta heads for the lady's room to read her a book, not without wondering who might that man be? He looks elegant, cultured and good looking, which hides his age as well as his previous marriages and his grown children, as old as or even older than Violeta herself. For now he doesn't care about social status, remembering he's the result of a similar situation. He asks Violeta out and takes her to a special place. She's rather uncomfortable having never been to such a luxurious place and feels the eyes of society's [44]fufurufas drilling her from behind. He's such a gentleman, always offering his arm. They have gone out quite often and had endless conversations. Violeta is

---

[44] Fufurufas: Snobbish, hoity-toity.

disconsolate, the day they have feared is here and the lady under her care has died. She's between a rock and a hard place, doesn't know whether to return to her town or look for another job. At the burial, she runs into the sculptor, who whispers into her ear to come find him outside the cemetery, he needs to talk to her. Violeta is hopeful about him but doesn't really think much about love, what she wants is to find another job, quickly. As she sees him arrive, her eyes light up and his nervous state is also evident. He confesses his love for her and wants to marry her. She is stunned as the last thing she expected was a "take it or leave it" proposal. She rushes her decision and accepts his proposal. They marry in a simple church, with few witnesses. She just sends a telegram to the village:

Come see me this Saturday.

Julia becomes worried over this telegram as she had just returned from picking up Martina Lucia. That same weekend they are unable to travel, the country is devastated by a terrible earthquake which causes thousands of deaths, collapsed buildings and in a split moment, entire towns have been reduced to rubble. They were felt all the way in their village.

Julia is still worried and wants to know, what was so urgent? The two months she had to wait to travel have felt very long. Violeta comes to pick them up at the bus station, accompanied by Marco and introduces him as her husband. Julia greets him courteously and waits for Violeta's story. They stay at the sculptor's house which is now Violeta's as well. Julia admires the house, every corner is different and feels like a museum. Wooden busts, some of his family and others of historical characters, all made by Marco.

They only stay for the weekend; Julia rushed her trip due to the urgency in the telegram but sees now it wasn't as urgent as she imagined. Julia tells her daughter it's time to go back to their routine. When they say goodbye, Violeta tells her mother she thinks it's time to have her daughter by her side. Julia breaks in tears and tells Violeta she'd rather die than be apart from the little girl. Even though she later tells her granddaughter she will stay with her mother. The three-year old refuses to stay and there's no way to tear her away from her grandma's dress. Violeta has to give up on wanting to keep the girl with her. Knowing how delicate her health is, she thinks to herself:

«*I rather she stay away than get sick, maybe when she's a bit older*».

Martina Lucia celebrates her four years of age and, of course, there's a memorable photograph of the event. At that young age she knows how to read and write, the dolls her mother bought are untouched, simply decorating the bed.

The house is emptying slowly, Margarita decided overnight to marry the businessman who visited the store where she worked. The store's son married a young woman of his same Quiché ethnicity. Catarino falls in love with a pastor's daughter, from the largest evangelical church in the village and ends up marrying her. Arturo leaves his military commissioner job because Martina gets so scared that she ends up under the bed every time he is drunk and starts shooting his guns into the air.

Many evangelizing events take place in the village and one day a very young pastor shows up at the house. He shares The Word of God and the first one who chooses to accept it is Arturo. Now that there's room in the house, he offers a bedroom to the pastor who turns the hallways into a makeshift church. Julia is annoyed by the noise until, one night, God touches her heart and she accepts The Word as well., seeing it as an opportunity to vindicate her life. Martina does not take her First Communion anymore since she is growing in the Christian religion; the godparents are upset with the family due to this decision and if, before it they hardly ever visited her, much less now.

Martina Lucia grows quickly, one of her great virtues is her love of animals, so her grandfather gifts her a pet on her sixth birthday.

The pup's seller warns him that, being a newborn, it could die easily; grandpa doesn't pay much attention, all he wants is to see his granddaughter's face when she sees the German shepherd. She can hardly believe her eyes and runs to hug her puppy. She still drinks her milk from a bottle, though out of sight of her grandparents who tease her:

"Such a big girl and still drinking milk from a bottle!"

Julia has fresh milk delivered to her door, which she boils with mint and cinnamon to keep it from making her granddaughter sick. Martina picks her oldest nursing bottle for her dog Kaliman. She divides the milk in half and jumps on the bed together with the dog to drink their milk together. Half of whatever she eats she shares with Kaliman. She picked that name because she heard an old radio serial on Arturo's old radio and she liked it for her dog.

Violeta is pregnant and feeling alone, sometimes. Most of the time, Marco is away, traveling for exhibitions of the busts he makes, inside and outside the country. Violeta has never liked going with him and it's been one of many arguments they've had. Marco is very finicky about his things, especially his shop, which Violeta cannot enter when he is there. When inspiration strikes, he only gets whatever he can for food and gets lost in his art. When Martina visits, Marco forgets his touchiness.

They have fully connected, he seems to see her as a diamond in the rough, just like he was. Marco wants to polish her, he is determined to teach her good manners. They study together and Marco gives her time and lessons. As if he were her father, he explains:

—A proper, educated and refined person always shows respect towards others.

With clear examples:

—When you have your soup, you move the spoon to your mouth, not your mouth to the spoon and don't slurp the soup or any drink… you'll attract attention and that's rude in front of someone else, don't do anything you wouldn't want done to you. Don't speak with your mouth full, like a pig, eat slowly for good digestion.

Martina listens intently, she is a good pupil and learns a lot from her tutor.

He teaches her to love the arts and to defend culture. Marco perceives elegance in her walk, elegance that no one has taught her. Without realizing it, this highlights her ancestry's heritage and like the saying goes: *"What is inherited is not stolen"*.

Marco loves talking to Martina as if she were an adult, when she is only six years old. Sometimes he can be a harsh taskmaster.

Desperately, he wants to pass on his knowledge to someone who can put them into practice. He's certain he has chosen the right person to keep alive good manners, love for the arts and for keeping the traditional customs and traditions alive. Marco watches Martina closely, every time he teaches her and thinks:

«I shall deposit my knowledge in her, I don't want to die without sowing a seed of change and I am sure that neither principles nor values will die. Her generation will be different!»

Marco wishes that Violeta would educate herself, like her daughter. He sometimes loses his patience before her refusal, not paying attention to what he shares and turns cold and sarcastic. In his anger, he calls her a small town yokel and although he apologizes, the damage is done.

Violeta goes into labor and is taken to the private hospital, already paid by Marco, to deliver her baby.

—it's a girl!

Says the attending physician.

The baby doesn't have any features from either of them, she is identical to Marco's mother. She was a woman of Kaqchikel ethnicity, married to a ladino and both rest in peace. Marco has forgotten his mother's tongue due to the discrimination he experienced as a schoolboy. When he talks with Martina he always emphasizes she should never be ashamed of her roots. Sad over his inability to rescue his roots, he's become resentful of society. With tears in his eyes he tells Martina:

—My mother was a victim of discrimination and my father the target of ridicule. They died loving each other and they gave me a life lesson: love knows no color or social classes.

Martina listens and kisses his hand. She has a really good time with her mother and Marco but is impatient to return home. Of course there is a vast difference between the two places and she prefers nature's freedom over four cement walls.

Marco baptizes the new baby as Luisa, to honor his mother. After two years, Violeta gets pregnant again. She has another baby girl, baptized as Jimena.

Violeta reminds Julia again over registering the little girl in school. Julia does so years later and Martina starts school at eight years of age. Her first day was not very pleasant. It's recess and all the other girls rush to the schoolyard. Martina doesn't know anyone and decides to stay in class to eat the delicious [45]pirujo con frijoles her grandmother made for her and put in her

---

[45] Pirujo con frijoles: a black bean sandwich. Pirujo is Guatemalan slang for a common type of bread. Black beans are ground into a paste. This is probably the most popular snack in Guatemala.

backpack. She wants to finish the little sticks for homework. As the bell rings, to signal recess is over, her classmates return to the classroom. One of them cleans the blackboard and throws the eraser at Martina's head. She gets up from her desk and with a frown, grabs her by the pigtails and slams her head against the blackboard. Sometimes children are the reflection of their parents and they, unconsciously, project it onto other children and that's how violence continues its cycle. Martina has been educated by Marco but also by her grandmother, who has taught her to never ever allow herself to be victimized especially if her rights are violated without reason. Her grandmother insists she must defend herself with tooth and nails even but never let anyone touch a hair on her head. The teacher brings her to the principal's office, striking Martina with a ruler, perpetuating inequality and injustice. Martina glares at her with fury in her eyes, for she is very unfair by punishing only her. She's never been struck at home but she cannot defend herself from her teacher, as her grandmother has told her. Without crying, she endures the pain caused by the ruler but without taking her eyes off the teacher. That same day, the teacher trips in the classroom and breaks her ankle; she looks at Martina and is afraid of her. After two weeks in first grade she is promoted to second grade, since she already knows how to read and write.

    Just before she started school, she no longer had a nanny. The young woman who has cared for her since she was one year old has health issues and tells Julia she cannot take care of the girl anymore. Julia doesn't understand why she tells her this, until that point they've gotten along and she's had no complaint of her excellent work. She's trusted her enough to leave Martina with her for days, when she's had to travel someplace. The woman tells her since she visited her sister, she's not feeling well. She tells her that her own sister has confessed how envious she was, of everything she achieved, going as far as getting pregnant by deceiving her boyfriend into cheating with her. She tells her how she never again got close to the young man, who's still in love with her, which her own sister cannot stand. Julia replies she still does not understand why she wants to quit her job. The woman continues telling her how her sister called her to make amends and offered her a glass of milk. She drank it gladly and when she gave the glass back the sister laughed mockingly. Crying, she tells her what happened:

    —Doña Julita! I really thought she wanted to mend things between us, I've never taken anything from her, quite the contrary, what little I had I gave to her and she even took my boyfriend. Since that time in her house I feel dizzy and keep vomiting. I hallucinate and sometimes I don't even remember who I am.

Julia hugs her and says:

—Oh my God! What that miserable gave you was pig's milk. She ruined your life, my dear. I have no remedy to fix that.

The young woman stops working and in her few lucid moments, she seeks Julia. They cry each time they see each other until one day, she goes completely mad and wanders around the village. Martina cried so much the last time she saw her nanny, who barely remembers her and in the midst of madness still tells her she loves her so much. From that day on, Martina didn't ever want another nanny.

She spends her vacations at her mother's house in the capital city, where she doesn't much like being away from her grandparents but is attracted by Marco's teachings. Martina loves her sisters; Luisa has dark skin, like her paternal grandmother did; Jimena is the opposite, very much like her father, with the skin color her paternal grandfather had. Martina returns full of new knowledge from each vacation. She doesn't want to return to school, her classmates whisper behind her back, afraid to say in front of her, but she can understand what they say and wonders why they call her bastard, orphan and even [46]india

---

[46] India lamida: a common racist insult.

lamida.

Marco asks:

—Who says this?

—And she responds:

—My classmates in school, they whisper among themselves.

Somewhat upset over the insults, Marco explains:

—Bastard: is a pejorative for someone born outside of a marriage. Orphan: someone who has no father or mother, or both. India lamida: India is a country in the Asian continent and her inhabitants are called Indians or Hindus; lamida means being skinny or an animal's lick.

Innocently, Martina thinks about Marco's words:

«*I have a mom... hmm, but no father. So I am a bastard, my mom is alive but I don't know if my father is, so I'm not sure if I'm an orphan; I'm not Indian, since I'm not from India but I am lamida because I'm so skinny I look like a skeleton and Kaliman licks me all the time... Hmmm... I really don't get it*»

Marco notices she seems to be deep in thought and she says:

—I don't understand much but I have a question, I will ask mom.

Marco doesn't really tell her the true meaning of the words her classmates use against her. He thinks how cruel human beings can be, at such a young age, prompted by their own parents. Julia comes to pick her up again although she doesn't want to return to the village or the school; however, her love for her grandparents makes her give in. Children forget most incidents quickly, as it happens to Martina, who sometimes forgets what happens in school.

In the afternoons she plays with the neighborhood's kids when suddenly a taxi stops and asks her:

—[47]Nena! Are you Violeta's daughter?

Martina runs away and asks:

—Why?

—So that you give her a message.

Martina pays close attention and tells him:

—Don't even talk to me, I don't talk to strangers, I'm telling my dad!

And runs to the door of her house.

The man goes on his way, thinking this girl looks a lot like one of his other daughters. He wants to know for sure if she is Violeta's daughter and therefore, his daughter. Martina mentions the incident to her grandma, when a man in a taxicab asked if she was Violeta's daughter. Julia is left wondering:

«*Who could be that man, the girl is telling me*

---

[47] Nena: Colloquial Guatemalan term of endearment for young girls.

about?»

Not everything in Martina's life is rose-colored. She had mumps and Julia placed some papaya leaves with lemon slices and coffee, held by a bandage made from a handkerchief. Other times she bleeds from her nose but what really worries Julia is not knowing why she has pain in her ear. Not all the time but when she gets it, spends days in bed under sedation, since the pain is so strong regular analgesics are not enough sometimes. In those desperate moments only her grandfather can heal her. Arturo carries her around the block a few times until she falls asleep. Her grandma places onion stalks on her which help relieve the pain a little. Those are the days when the grandparents suffer next to her because sometimes they don't know how to help her.

In the afternoons she goes out to play with the neighbors and one day she doesn't wear shoes. Her grandmother doesn't notice when she goes out in sandals. She has always told her that those are only for inside the house and that she must wear shoes out in the street. They're playing with a ball and it goes among the bushes. Martina runs to get it and they only hear a scream from her.

The grandparents run out as quickly as they can to see what happened, the kids are scared and say maybe a snake bit her. They check her foot and Arturo notices her toe is red and swollen, Julia touches her forehead and in a matter of seconds she is burning with fever. Desperate, her grandfather carries her at a quick pace to the [48] IGSS with Julia behind them, crying all the way. When they arrive, her whole foot is swollen and red and she is almost passed out. The doctor asks what happened, the grandparents tell him what they know. After checking her, the doctor tells them they arrived in the nick of time, because he was barely able to contain the venom from spreading to her heart. Whichever animal bit her is unknown, some guessed perhaps it was the mythical [49]cara de niño or a black widow spider. It wasn't a snake bite. This was a huge scare for the grandparents, however, they didn't stop her from going out to play, although now with all precautions. She never again went out without shoes.

Martina is an excellent student since her reward is traveling to the capital city and her stays are extended to every three months.

It's Christmas season and Martina celebrates her tenth birthday at Marco's house.

Julia wants to suspend the quarterly trip as

---

[48] IGSS: Instituto Guatemalteco de Seguridad Social (Guatemalan Institute of Social Security); community hospitals/clinics around the country.
[49] Cara de niño: literally "child's face" a local variety of potato bug, a fearsome looking insect, assumed to be poisonous; it is completely harmless.

times have turned dangerous but Martina insists she wants to go. There's many revolts after the latest coup d'etat which force Martina to stay a few days longer. Martina watches Marco, stuck to the news, doesn't interrupt him and heads for the bookcase, looking for one that catches her eye. They are soon drawn by one called "The Prince" which she leafs through and then places back among the others. Marco turns off the radio and goes to her. Previously he gave her the novel "Maria" and hasn't had the chance to ask:

—Did you like your gift?

As she leafs through another book, she replies:

—I liked it a lot! I started it already.

He tells her:

—Any book you like from there, you can take.

Marco is very punctual about his habits and, book in hand, he reminds Martina it is time for tea. Together, they head for the living room. Suddenly, he doesn't feel well and drops his cup and grabs his chest. Martina screams for her mother, scared, and Violeta runs quickly to see what happened. Seeing her husband on the floor, she calls an ambulance and tries to give first aid. Marco didn't have time to say goodbye, a heart attack has just ended his life.

To the wake came Marco's oldest sons,

dressed like crows, they shed no tears and, like buzzards, only looked at Violeta from head to toe. At the cemetery, without any respect for her pain or their dead father, they present her with documents saying she must leave the house. In the midst of her sadness, she rents a truck and loads her belongings. They watch her like rapacious birds and don't allow her to remove any busts, paintings or anything of value. She is not interested in any of that but they're things she acquired with her husband and whatever they built together, belongs to her daughters. However, she only takes her daughter's furniture and a few other things for which she has written proof of ownership. They take over everything, never having worked for it and have no compassion for their sisters, who are left orphaned at an early age.

Violeta returns to her village. On the way there she remembers the dream she once had and how none of it came true. Tears flow from her eyes and stops reminiscing because that also brings back some of the worst moments of her life. She wipes her tears away and thanks God for her daughters' life.

She moves into her parents' house and starts yet again. With her few savings she starts a small corner store and makes her way in life. Martina is simply devastated by the death of someone she considered a father figure, crying in her room next to her faithful companion. She hugs the doll that Marco gave her in one of her birthdays, remembering the happy moments by his side, the long learning talks and a few moments of bad temper. Having her mother and sisters near her relieves her sadness a bit.

Returning from the market, the rapist finds Violeta one day and questions her:

—You disappeared from the village and now you're going to answer my questions.

She looks at him with hatred in her eyes and says:

—I'm not answering any questions to you, you damned bastard!

He continues saying:

—The oldest girl, is she my daughter?

Furiously, she tells him no. He insists saying he will take her to have a paternity test done. Violeta looks him straight in the eye and warns him that, if he goes anywhere near her daughter, she will kill him with her own hands. She makes it clear she is no longer the girl he raped one day. He realizes she is not playing around when she says this. From that time on, he ceased stalking them.

Whatever little learning Martina got from Marco, she practices every day so as not to forget it and to be able to teach her children, as he used to tell her. She remembers him all the time, as when he said:

"Good breeding is inherited but it must be practiced; in other cases you learn and all the same, it must be practiced, so that you don't forget it".

Martina loves playing basketball. Her grandmother scolds her each time she shows up with skinned knees, when she trips on the court. In hopes of making her stop playing, Julia applies peroxide, wipes fairly hard and applies merthiolate and sulfa powder. Martina almost passes out from the burning and the pain but won't stop playing and her grandma won't stop giving her the same treatment.

Martina has become good friends with a sixth grade girl who lives nearby, they both love playing basketball. Every morning, Martina picks her friend up on her way to school and without fail, Kaliman the guardian joins them. Since Martina started school, the dog walks with her to school and has learnt, from her grandfather, to pick her up when school's out. Just from looking at Kaliman, no one dares go near the girls, especially when he shows his huge fangs.

One Friday morning around eleven, they send all students home early without telling them why. Martina hides in the bathroom with her friend and when they see everyone's left, they come out to play feeling like they own the court, no one bothers them. They hear buzzing nearby which they ignore. In front of the school there's a military detachment and shots are heard. They think it's the firecrackers celebrating the inauguration of the village's new butcher shop when they hear their names; it's Arturo and her friend's father. They give them directions to get out through the back and try to figure out how to get them out of that mess. The girls are scared at being found out, having no idea whatsoever of the magnitude of the situation happening that day. They get out of school and heading each one to their home, they notice it's a ghost town. On both sides of the street there's columns of soldiers. Rumor spreads that the village has been taken over by guerrillas. The buzzing they heard was bullets fired at bank robbers, which created panic and confusion among the population. Martina's life has a marked difference to her ancestors' generations. Julia knows Martina has the gift of her father, Demesio and her mother Martina's elegance; she doesn't want that heritage to continue on her generation except for the mother's side.

Martina learns so much from Julia, her kitchen secrets and even learns how to make tortillas. She repeats the same thing to her that she used to say to her sister Victoria: to start a great day, one has to start by making the bed. She teaches her to be tidy and many secrets more. Added to Marco's teachings she is completing her formation as a good, well rounded human being, just like he wanted.

Martina spends her time reading, on a swing Arturo made for her under the mango tree. On her grandfather's land there are many fruit trees such as zapote, whose harvest is already sold when the season comes; a nance tree that Arturo ends up cutting down due to all the dried leaves it created; banana, coffee, cacao, and grandma's orchard.

On the lands impounded from Arturo there's a huge plantain plantation, which they're cleaning slowly. They have just cut many trees, leaving the trunks near Arturo's property. In her playtimes with the neighbors, Martina makes up new games, as always. This time she comes up with another one. They place the trunks one after the other, like building a road. They start walking on them and whoever falls, gets a [50]coscorrón. They've done it a few times, making a big hubbub as each one gets to the end without falling. In one of those times Martina suddenly slips and only can place her arm to protect her face. She feels something warm near her wrist and sees it bleeding profusely; her little friends scamper, scared and screaming, to let Julia know. Martina cut her hand with a broken bottle, of which there's plenty around the trunks;

---

[50] Coscorrón: rap on the head; noogie.

her grandmother dresses her wound, just like she did with her skinned knees. The cut was big and deep, leaving a huge scar. The land is cleared, some say the land will be developed into lots and the greenery becomes more and more scarce.

During mango season Martina breaks her handmade clay piggy-bank, in the shape of an owl. In it, she saved the twenty-five cents Julia gives her every day as an allowance to buy snacks or whatever she wants in school. She has an idea and takes out her savings to make it happen. She joins Julia going to the market and buys small bags of [51]chile cobán, [52]pepitoria, lime and salt. She cuts a few mangoes from the tree, some still very green, others [53]zarazos and a few ripe ones. She prepares bags of sliced mangoes, puts a table out and tells her sister Luisa that, if she tends their table, she will give her a percentage of sales, which she accepts. The business fails since her little sister eats all the mango bags instead of selling them. She buys a new piggy-bank, in the shape of a dog like Kaliman and thinks:

«I better keep on saving my [54]lenes, I'm better off»

---

[51] Chile Cobán: a type of wild chile, named after the city of Cobán, where it is grown
[52] Pepitoria: roasted and ground pumpkin seeds.
[53] Zarazo: neither green nor ripe or just beginning to ripen.
[54] Lenes: Guatemalan slang for Centavos (cents)

Martina joins the school's basketball team, much to Julia's chagrin. After much insistence, she allows her to go play in the surrounding municipalities, where they face other schools' teams. They have tournaments between male and female teams. Martina's eyes are irresistibly drawn to a boy playing for the all-male school. She tells her best friend that she's going to marry him when she grows up and laughs out loud at Elizabeth's expression, as if gagging. Since she's disgusted by almost everything she only tells Martina:

—[55]Chishhh!

Martina laughs and adds, only to upset her more:

—He's so cute!

Every time there's another tournament, she only sighs for that mystery boy.

In the last year of elementary, she studied hard as never before, she wanted the best grades. She doesn't understand what's happening in the country and why they send the students home without a date for returning during the current school cycle. There's an ongoing teachers' strike and the government cannot come to an agreement with them. All students are made to pass that school year. This makes her so mad, having given her all to studying only to be given a pass grade by

---

[55] Chish: common, old fashioned expression of disgust.

decree.

After Violeta and her sister's stay at the house, Martina is left without any dolls; they're all missing their heads. That upsets her quite a lot because one of those she saved as a memento from someone who was a father figure, teacher and friend to her: Marco. She asks Julia for a lock for her room, which she's never had to use before but given that her sisters destroy everything they touch, she decides to do this from now on. Even though it will only be for a short time until Violeta finishes building her house on property inherited from her father. The house is empty once again as the church moves to a different location and Violeta moves to her new house with her girls.

A new phase in her education begins for Martina Lucia, who finds Elizabeth after a few months of not seeing each other, in the same new school and classroom. This is a new experience since now it's not only their old classmates from the all-girl school they attended together but also from all the other schools, now thrown together in a coed middle school. Martina blushes when she sees the boy she likes. Elizabeth elbows her when he comes closer to them. He introduces himself and tells them it will be an honor to attend school together with them. This was only a fleeting crush for Martina, since he has a girlfriend in another classroom. After this heartbreak, she won't be interested in anyone else.

Kaliman now knows the way to the new school to go find Martina, at first he was confused and used to head for the old school.

Violeta is still a very attractive woman with many pretenders but her priority is her daughters. Among those pretenders there's a very good looking man but she pays him no heed. He's a widower who just buried his wife and that started problems between his children and Violeta, through no fault of her own. This man's daughter-in-law declared war on her, also, even though she knew Violeta's views about him. For a little while, things settle down with this woman.

Arturo and Julia have always tried to give Martina the best they can. She's so happy for the grandparents she has and hopes one day to have a lucky turn in life so that she can pay them back for everything they did for her. She wishes they lack for nothing for, over the years, she sees their strength and faculties diminishing. With no malice, Martina figures out a strategy to make money. She draws a few coffee beans from the sacks her grandfather has readied for sale. From those she gathers about a pound of coffee and sells it. She's paid about half the true market price but she thinks this is right.

When her grandfather delivers the coffee he notices the missing grams in each sack, scratching his head and swearing he weighed them himself to the right weight.

He replenishes each sack to the top but remains doubtful. When it's time for the next shipment he hides and watches. Martina shows up with a pail and coolly proceeds to slide her slender fingers through the stitches on the sides. She jumps when Arturo catches her in the act. He takes her by the hand, sits down and stiff as a board, lays her across his lap. He spanks her as he says:

—A granddaughter of mine does not take anything without permission, that is stealing and I did not raise a thief. If you need anything, you have a mouth. Ask for it, nothing's ever been denied to you.

Even as he spanks her, the grandfather cries. He's never raised a hand to her other than for caressing her and it hurts his soul to have to strike the apple of his eyes. Martina won't stop crying, not because of pain but she has never been so severely punished. Soon after she has a burning fever and Julia places cool rubbing alcohol compresses on her forehead. Fever's gone down and sighing deeply, she falls asleep.

The next day Arturo approaches her, looking sad, seeing his little girl in bed due to the spanking she got from him. She hugs him and sobbing asks for forgiveness, she swears she didn't know that was such a grave fault and promises that she will never again touch anything without permission, which she does from that day forward.

Every time Julia goes across the border, Martina hands her a list of things to bring. The first few times Julia raised a ruckus but eventually got used to it, telling herself she has no one else to spoil and Martina is the only one to brighten her life.

The cashier at the market knows her already and makes her task easier, finding the candy for her granddaughter. One day she tells her:

—If you like, give me the list and I will find it all for you, while you do your regular shopping.

Julia thanks her for the gesture and hands over the list.

Beautiful mommy, today it's only a few things:
Duvalines, the usual little box.
Maria's or Animal Cookies
Carlos V, also the little box.
Cornflex
Nido Milk, Kaliman likes it a lot
Chocomilk, gansitos
Any Sabritas at all.
That's all lovely mommy. Hide them well so that customs doesn't find them. I love you with all my soul and when I'm older and I can work you won't have to.

Martina

The cashier is crying and laughing at the same time when she reads Martina's adorable letter. When Julia pays for her purchases, she tells her it's been a joy helping her get all her requests.

She has one last question and asks:

—Who is Kaliman?

And Julia answers it is her granddaughter's dog.

The girl only smiles and tells her she hopes some day she can meet her lovely granddaughter. Julia thinks to herself:

«*Adorable?? A spoiled brat she is! If only she knew her...*»

And says goodbye, shaking her head in wonder.

When Julia returns home, they're all awaiting her. Kaliman wags his tail, knowing there's something for him as well. With hugs and kisses, Martina, thanks her grandma for her generosity and tells her that, for one week, she will go to the mill. It's not far from their house and on the first day Julia warns her:

—Don't take the dog, whenever anyone gets too close to you he wants to bite their arms off; do not put your hands inside the mill, it doesn't matter if it's not running, don't stay tattling with the other girls at the corner store.

She answers:

—Yes, mommy... all right!

And to the dog:

—You, Kaliman! Wait here until I come back.

The dog looks at her and blinks, letting her know he understood.

When she's almost at the mill she sees a woman she half recognizes, who's also come to grind some corn. With the bucket for the [56]masa she hits Martina on her right side. Martina cusses her out with a rude gesture and continues on her way since the bump wasn't that bad. When she returns home she tells Julia what happened:

—You see, mamaíta, the daughter-in-law of that man who was courting with my mommy, hit me with her bucket, here.

Pointing at her right side where Julia untucks her blouse to confirm how bad it was. Martina says it doesn't hurt. Julia regrets telling her not to take the dog. That same afternoon, Martina is once again burning with fever and it won't go away. Violeta learns about this incident and goes straight to complain to the man, warning him that if something happens to her daughter, no human power will keep her from wiping out his entire family. He has no idea what she is talking about until she explains.

---

[56] Masa: Corn dough.

After one week, Martina's condition worsens. The best doctor in the village suggests they take her to the state hospital at the provincial capital. At the hospital, they take an X-ray of the affected area. Martina's right kidney shows a black shadow, which the doctors cannot diagnose. She is immediately admitted to the hospital, for observation, after controlling her fever with medication. Each day the shadow grows, covering her kidney and Martina has no respite from the pain. Julia and Violeta are worried over the confused doctors, who cannot provide an accurate diagnosis. They've tried antibiotics to control possible infections but it made no difference. They go visit a folk healer, a really good one who knows their affliction as soon as she sees them. With a soft voice she tells them:

—She's strong and her destiny is a great one, she has guardians around her.

They greet each other as they come in. Julia bows and says:

—My father was your teacher and I know you're no quack.

The woman extends her hand towards where they should sit and says:

—I learned a lot from Tata Demesio but let's cut to the chase. Your girl has The Gift and she cannot be beat, she will soon have the cure. The woman who did this wants to hurt her because she is your firstborn.

Looking straight at Violeta, she continues:

—What that woman doesn't know is that everything they do to Tata's heiress will come back to her tripled. No need to do anything, her own energy protects her... your eyes shall see!

She lights white candles and finishes saying:

—The girl has her own [57]nahual, go in peace, it's not her time. This reading has no cost to you, it's already been paid.

They say goodbye and Julia is more altered than before because, what she didn't want known, the woman has revealed.

Two weeks without a diagnostic go by until the hospital's director says they must operate. The black spot has covered almost the entire kidney and they need to remove it before it extends to other vital organs. That day, a young doctor visits Martina and she tells him, with a weak voice:

—You're the one who's going to heal me, right?

He laughs and taking out a pill tells her:

—I'm only the intermediary to bring your medicine; take this pill, I will visit you every morning for the next three days.

She looks at the pill and with great effort swallows what looks like a large black suppository; the young doctor leaves her room and

---

[57] Nahual: Protecting animal spirit or energy, totem.

she falls asleep.

Surgery is scheduled sometime over the next three days. Two have passed and the doctors are shocked to see the next X-ray. Almost ¾ of the kidney has been cleared and the operation is suspended, they have no explanation for it. At eight the next morning the young doctor shows up again with the pill and tells Martina:

—Good morning! My little sickie is looking better, here's the last pill you're taking and in a few days you'll go back home. I must go but I will always be near you.

Still weak, Martina stutters her thanks. About nine that same morning, another medical team comes to see her due to her unusual condition and they want to watch her closely. Half dazed Martina says:

—More doctors?

As they look at each other and the hospital's director asks her:

—My child, why do you say that?

She tells him the young doctor, who gave her the black pill, had just left. They don't understand which doctor she's talking about, since all the doctors in the hospital are right there to learn about her condition.

She describes the young doctor:

—He dresses like you, is younger than you. Mmm... he's very tall, looks like those guys on

TV.

They talk and agree there is no such young doctor among themselves or the residents. They draw blood to determine what medication she received and the only result is an excess of vitamin K and a healthy kidney. The hospital director, failing to solve the mystery, discharges her without saying another word. The next day she returns home and celebrates her fourteenth birthday. The woman who tried to harm her had a miscarriage and never had any other children after that while her family goes from one tragedy to another. As the saying goes:

"you get what you deserve" especially when an innocent creature's life is in danger, no human can stop heavenly justice.

Having finished the school year, Martina breaks down when saying goodbye to her best friend. It's time for destiny to take them along different paths. Elizabeth promises to be at Martina's celebration of her fifteen years before going to the capital city. Violeta is combing Martina for the day of celebration of her fifteen years of age.

Behind her ear she finds a spot, a birthmark coming down the generations through Demesio's lineage. Violeta is scared and calls her mother to show her the spot. Julia tells her she searched her over and over when she was a baby and couldn't find it, never imagined it would be well hidden there. She confesses it is the birthmark of the chosen ones, the ones getting The Gift through her father's descendants. This settles Violeta down a little bit for, since Martina's illness, every little unknown thing scares her. Julia continues telling her that there's another birthmark that denotes their grandmother's genes and that's the mole by their lips. Violeta tells her that Martina's is not on her lips but the side of her neck. Laughing, she tells Julia:

—Her genes are strong, [58]mamaíta! Of papaíto we only got the high cheekbones, big ears and good nature.

Martina is entertained by their talk but reminds them, with a laugh, that they must hurry, their guests will arrive shortly. The neighbors, some friends from school and certainly her best friend are the special guests. School's out on vacation and it's also time for the village fair.

Most people are occupied with other activities and, while Martina would have loved inviting everybody, it really was a simple affair, only to mark the day. The hospital bills took a toll on the family finances. After the party she throws

---

[58] Mamaíta/papaíto: literally "little mommy/daddy" – it's a Guatemalan quirk to make everything "little" as a term or expression of endearment. Most everything gets the treatment simply by adding "ito" or "ita" at the end.

herself on her bed joined by her faithful friend. This was a tiring day and she feels the tiredness gave her a deep pain in her abdomen and she asks Julia for some tea, for the pain, and stays in bed, exhausted.

The next morning, the dog is altered, coming and going from the room. Martina still sleeps but Kaliman's whine wakes her up. She's still in pain and sits on the edge of the bed, stretching her arms. She thanks God, like every morning. She addresses the dog telling him:

—Now what, Kaliman! What's your problem, why won't you let me sleep?

Te dog climbs into her bed and sniffs around, like he's searching for something. Martina tells him to get off the bed, she's going to make it. When she's doing the bed, she screams in fright and right away Julia is at her side asking:

—What happened, mija?

Martina tells her grandma the bed seems to be all bloody. Martina checks Kaliman to ensure it's not him that's hurt.

Julia laughs and explains what's happening:

—I was going to take you to the doctor one of these days, because you were late to this…

As she can't stop herself from laughing and continues:

—Even the poor [59]chucho is all scared, no

---

[59] Chucho: Guatemalan slang for 'dog'

wonder he's all excited!

Grandma goes to buy some red pills to ease the cramps that puberty is giving Martina. The red spots prove her monthly torture, her abdominal cramps getting worse each time. Her grandma tries to give her relief with the red pills and warm water bags, which she places on her belly. There's time when nothing helps and she stays in bed for a few days.

Martina still goes with Arturo to church although Julia only seldom goes with them. The church events are growing in scale, this time the evangelists have come from far. It's the first night of revival and Martina sits almost at the far end, together with other young girls. As one of the guest preachers begins his sermon, calling on them to repent, Martina rises from her seat and heads to the altar, hands held high. When he is in front of the pastor, she starts speaking in tongues as the congregation listens in silence.

The **pastor** calls one of his fellow preachers who has the gift of interpreting. He starts translating what she is saying:

—I am your lord and I am coming soon! This young woman has been granted the gifts of healing and speaking words of justice; she shall walk barefoot to wear my sandals; you will see her in rags for she has not worn my tunic; I shall crown her when she fulfills her promise… the ministry awaits her. For you, man of faith, do not waste your stay in this place and deliver the baptism of the waters to my daughter, for your eyes have seen the baptism in the Holy Spirit.

Martina opens her eyes, confused about what she's doing in front of the altar, drenched in sweat. They seat her in the front pew and bring her some water. That day, there was healing!

Arturo tells her all this and she replies she's only fifteen, too young to be baptized. He only answers that she must obey God's designs. Sunday morning the baptism is celebrated in the usually very cold waters of the river. When Martina wades in she says:

—The water is warm!

Others come in after her, who will also receive baptism and they confirm the water is nice. Martina wants to go into the ministry but Julia doesn't allow it. She reminds her that, first, she must graduate and have a career. Even though Martina tried convincing her that the ministry is, indeed, a career, Julia is unmoved. Martina decides to study to be a school teacher at the nearest such school, which is in the provincial capital. Luckily her aunt Margarita lives there and she moves in with her.

Armed conflict is at an all-time high; buses are checked both by the army and the guerrillas, even by customs officers, all looking for contraband.

Martina travels each week, she misses her grandparents and her dog, who couldn't join her, so every Saturday morning, she comes back home and travels back to her aunt's on Monday morning. Luckily, her classes are in the afternoon. Julia is very uneasy about the checkpoints in the highways so the trips are shortened to once a month, with Julia coming to see her also one other time. Martina attends the national school at the provincial capital; before the end of classes, the building was taken over by young men explaining that as long as they follow orders, no one would be hurt. The country is in chaos as a consequence of constant student kidnappings by different political ideologies.

Martina is not scared by the event, on the contrary, she consoles her classmates, some in a real panic. The frightened parents start arriving at the school when she spots her aunt and tells her everything is alright. Their captors allow students to receive food and goods from their parents. Margarita brought a blanket and some food for Martina. This is a very cold region and they don't know how long they will be held captive. They only release the students the next day. Martina, protected by her guardians, still doesn't realize the scope of how they live and suffer in the outside world, until that black month of August.

It got into Martina's head to head for the United States when she turned eighteen. The country's situation gets more chaotic by the day but she also wants to improve her financial life and maybe change her generation's fate. Her spirit has been empowered and she starts working on an armor of mental strength. But also her physical state and she signs up for karate lessons; she continues playing basketball, swims and also signs up for the army reserve.

One of her school teachers is a volunteer fireman and stops by the station before teaching his classes. Martina needs help with homework due to a missed day and he tells her to look for him at the fire station, that he will bring them to her. She stops by the following morning to pick up the assignments. The teacher introduces her to his mates and she offers her services as a volunteer to help them out, since the mess in their office is complete. Once a week she comes over to arrange and file the office paperwork, making them very happy that she is supporting them.

A new private school opens in town also offering a teaching degree, Julia telling Martina to sign up there. Martina wants to remain at her school and finish her degree there. This new school is very expensive and she wants to save as much as possible for her trip. No one knows about her idea, which she's had in mind for a while. Her week is packed with activities, with a full calendar:

Monday through Friday from one to six in the afternoon, she has regular school classes; Monday mornings she volunteers at the fire station; Tuesday and Thursday mornings she has karate lessons; Wednesday mornings are for basketball practice; Friday, early mornings, she walks to the pools, where she swims; all day Saturday, army reserve classroom instruction and Sunday, all day, military drills. Every day she grows stronger physically, emotionally and mentally, for her MIGRANT DESTINY.

One of those Saturdays she is called in by the army reserve commander. He indicates her identification document is missing from her file, to which she replies smiling that she doesn't have it yet; he asks for her birth certificate and she smiles again and tells him it's in her school registration. In reality, she's trying to hide that she is still underage. Her lies are believable since she is a big girl and this makes her look older. The commander suggests she better get a copy or he won't be able to certify her course completion. What really interests her is to get the training to improve her physique and her mind. She has the face of a girl in a woman's body and she forgets about the document.

After three weeks she is called again and this

time she worries because she's out of ideas to avoid presenting the required document. The commander asks her to represent them in a beauty pageant to which she replies she's not into that. She participated in one at her school last year and all it did was make her spend her savings. The commander insists and emphasizes they will cover all expenses. All other brigades in the military region have a [60]madrina to represent them.

Martina is a natural beauty, with an elegant poise, five foot three inches tall, with fair skin tanned by the sun, brown eyes and brown, curly hair like her father. She is the perfect candidate. Martina accepts with the condition she is not expelled from the reserves. An agreement is reached.

Preparations begin at the halls of the military headquarters for the zone, everything is different in that world. The contestants are treated like queens. Every young lady is quite beautiful, competition is hard-fought. Martina knows each one of them, some of whom are sweet with a good heart while others are quite arrogant.

In all the coming and goings, she's neglected her training and this worries her. She's unsure of being able to convince her grandma of completing

---

[60] Madrina: while the literal translation is "godmother" in this context the title is given to a young lady to serve as both a 'mascot' and delegate representing an organization, sometimes but not always, in a pageant or for PR purposes.

her degree in the current school or switching to the new private school. In the village she will not be able to train like she does in the provincial capital. All the young beauties look stunning, each one identified by a band representing each military brigade, Martina's reads:

"MADRINA OF ARMY RESERVES".

She doesn't really like the experience, she's tired of the rehearsals for the evening gala of the event. Entrances and exits, up and down the stairs to the stage have left her out of breath, so she decides to go out and get some fresh air. She's interested in exploring the encampment, the sky is lit by a huge full moon and the stars glitter like jewels. As she starts walking she hears heartrending cries. As her curiosity grows she nears the place where the moans are coming from and she stops for a moment to determine the direction where the lamentations are coming from. She thinks she can do something underground and hunkers down, almost kneeling. Then she hears a loud voice saying:

—Did you lose something?

She stands up at once and says:

—Good night, colonel! I believe I heard cries.

With an intimidating, creepy smile the colonel tells her it may be that underground there's a dungeon where traitors are tortured. She looks him in the eye and says they hear so much about them, that may even be true.

The colonel tells her the second part of the rehearsal is about to start and only she is missing. Fixing his red beret, ends the conversation telling her:

—Careful, gorgeous little girl... remember curiosity killed the cat.

As he continues laughing, as a warning.

She has no further doubts but has had enough for one night.

The event will take place in a few days and that weekend all the contestants are staying in a huge house, making final preparations and getting ready for it.

When the great day arrives Martina feels like she's choking out of the stress caused by seeing the huge hall full of people. All the ladies are in gowns and stunning hairdos. Martina lets her natural hair alone and has almost no makeup. Her dress is short, three inches above the knee; a black upper part with ¾ sleeves and a burnt pink satin skirt with three plies and shoes with a comfortable heel. She places among the top five finalists and her nervousness increases. The entire front section is made up of students from the military academy, which is her cheering squad since the instructors belong to the brigade she represents. She hears her name and is paralyzed, she doesn't want to fail them and thinks:

«You gotta be realistic… just placing among the top five is more than I expected».

She hears her name and steps to the front, where they ask her a question. In that moment, she loses her hearing, her vision turns blurry and from afar she hears her name again and that of her brigade in the students' voices and a few other fans. A few seconds have passed which feel like an eternity to her. There's an expectant silence filling that enormous hall awaiting her answer as she has the microphone and takes a deep breath to give her answer. Her nerves betray her and all they can hear is a 'thanks' echoing through every corner. Silence is overwhelming and she doesn't say another word. She looks at the students she represents and blows them a kiss, immediately turning around for she feels about to pass out. As soon as she exits the stage her cheering section stands up and starts clapping for her, which spreads to the entire attendance. Final results favor the girls who gave a whole speech as an answer and between her 'thanks' and the loud cheering she received, she finished in fourth place. From that day on she never again participated in another pageant.

After that pleasant experience Martina's life opens up to new adventures and experiences. She retakes her favorite activities. During classroom military instruction she's thanked by the officers for agreeing to represent them in the event and throw a little party in her honor. She hasn't been able to visit her family due to the weekend classes and drills. Being madrina has its perks, she's still treated like a queen and takes advantage of it by missing class one weekend. She tells her aunt she got permissions from the military and will be able to travel the following weekend. Friday afternoon she attends school and on her way back, to her surprise, her grandma has come to visit. She tells her she was planning on going the next day so her grandma answers that it's no problem, they can travel together the next morning.

Saturday morning she tells her:

—Mamaíta! Let me go real quick to the fire station to tell the guys I'm not coming Monday as usual and to ask if they want anything from the coast and then we go, ok?

Her grandma encourages to hurry back in time since the afternoons turn rainy quite often. She quickens her pace and when she arrives, the firemen are surprised, since it wasn't her day to go. She explains the reason for her visit and they laugh, telling her it will be a long list, for leaving them alone. They're all talking when Martina screams, everyone scrambles and asks her what's the matter? She tells them she felt a stab of pain on her right side of her abdomen. Martina holds it with her left hand and continues:

—I feel like a knife stabbed and it really hurts a lot.

They are paralyzed for a moment before one of them reacts:

—Quickly! We need to get her to the hospital, that's a symptom she has appendicitis!

Scared, Martina tells them she cannot go, she has to let them know at her house what's happening. They place her on a stretcher and stop by Margarita's house to notify her. Julia feels like dying herself to see her little girl on a stretcher again even as the firemen tell her she will be alright. Upon arrival she goes straight to the operating room. The attending physician indicates they brought her just in time, just a little more delay and she wouldn't have made it.

They ask for blood donations and Violeta goes to the military headquarters to explain what's happened to her and mentions they need blood donors. When the reserve company learns about this, one of the officers gathers a few soldiers and heads for the hospital. The decorated lieutenant, with his [61]Kaibil beret, walks ramrod straight through the hospital's hallways.

Looking desperate he asks for information about the condition of the battalion's madrina. His

---

[61] Kaibil: Special Forces of the Guatemalan Army.

eyes cannot hide the pain he feels; the fit young man, almost six feet tall, keeps on walking straight to the blood donation room. Orders the soldiers to line up and with glassy eyes tells the nurse:

—You take all the blood you need, I'd give my life if needed, for my queen!

The nurse asks for his blood type and he answers AB-. They draw all the blood they can since it's a hard-to-find type and very few people want to donate it. The nurse tells him:

—With this donation the young girl will be discharged!

The office, a little hazy and dizzy after giving blood asks her:

—My blood is for my queen, right?

The nurse replies, a little miffed, that the donation is for the hospital as a whole and can be given to any patient. He's shocked because he thought his blood was going to run through his beloved Madrina's veins only.

Disappointed, he goes to Martina's room. She still under sedation and does not notice his presence; he caresses her face as he kisses her forehead telling her:

—You scared me, pretty girl" You have no idea how much I love you.

The lieutenant never again expresses his feelings for Martina after that day; she never learned about his secret love for her.

After this, the doctor forbids any hard exertions for Martina so she takes this certificate to also be discharged from the reserves. She stops all her physical activities.

After six months the surgery has healed perfectly. Martina is in finals before the end of the school year. Every morning, Margarita prepares a thermos of basil tea, as recommended by Julia, according to her it is a great memory aid. After an intense week of final tests Martina is mentally exhausted and decides to go home and spend time with her dog.

She arrives Friday night after a two hour trip. Kaliman is beside himself at seeing her since she was not expected this weekend. Her grandfather receives a visit from the pastor and they overextend their chat, so knowing he lives on the other side of town, tells him that the dog will walk with him. Kaliman has been trained by Martina and Arturo and is obedient and smart, seems like the only thing he can't do is talk. Arturo gives him directions if he were a human being.

It's almost midnight, the time when the last pullman bus arrives from the capital city. At that time the dog is sniffing his way back home and while crossing the main street, the bus driver doesn't even realize he hit Kaliman. He doesn't survive the accident.

Witnesses say:

"It's don Arturito's dog, someone better go tell him"

After Kaliman's death Martina never again had another pet.

Monday morning she heads back to her aunt's, her heart heavy with sadness, with no desire to return but classes are not over yet. The bus is chock full of people. Martina always rides in the front seats and near the window because she cannot stand the smells produced by sweaty people huddled together. In the distance she spots a checkpoint and people in the bus worry. Some whisper "It's the guerrillas". The bus stops and is boarded by a few men with military pants and dark shirts; some have a red bandanna around their neck and wear black berets with a star in the middle.

One of them says:

—We're young rebels and all we want is whatever food you have.

Martina has a bag full of her favorite snacks and says:

—That black bag is mine, I have all my favorite snacks, you can take it.

People are stunned and no one says a word when it happens. That day Martina's wearing jeans, which she has altered to suit her style. She added a sideband of clothing pins, from large to small, making it look like mariachi trousers; one of the legs has holes which she covered with a red bandanna; holding it up she wears a black belt with a silver buckle. She wears a cutoff plaid blouse of black and white squares, with ¾ sleeves, almost showing her belly button; weird high top black sneakers with brightly colored laces, one yellow and one orange; her wrists sport lots of bracelets, some silver and the rest made of traditional textiles. In each finger she sports a silver ring; one earring dangles to her shoulder and the other one short. Half her hair is raised by another red bandanna, matching the one around her knee.

One of the rebels tells her:

—I like your style. It's pretty unique! When I eat one of your snacks I'll think of you.

She fixed him with a steady look into his bluish eyes.

They thank the bus riders for their courtesy and say goodbye with these words:

—Farewell and "hasta la Victoria siempre! Patria o Muerte!"

They have barely climbed the next incline inside the jungle mists when another checkpoint appears. After a wide curve with space to pull over the bus stops again. Two sour-faced soldiers climb in and order everyone off the bus. Men are separated from women and Martina recognizes one of the officers from the battalion she represented. He still hasn't seen her.

One of the soldiers tells her:

—What the hell are you looking at, over there? You look like a guerrilla to me!

Martina looks him up and down and with a smirk tells him:

—And you look like a fag, [62]cuque.

Suddenly he strikes with the [63]Galil's butt, knocking her wind out. She grabs her belly and sees something shine far up in the mountain, like a signal. The brute, angry soldier tells her:

—Repeat what you just said.

Martina raises her head and tells him:

—Do you see that shiny thing up there? They're only awaiting my signal to blow your officer's head off.

The soldier chambers his rifle and points at her head in front of the aghast riders and asks:

—How do you know he is an officer?

After a few seconds the officer tells her:

—Madrina!

And knocks the rifle away from her head and angrily asks:

—What in the hell are you doing, recruit? Don't you see she is our madrina?

The soldier turns white when he hears those

---

[62] Cuque: Guatemalan slang for a soldier.
[63] Galil: The Israeli IMI Galil was the regulation rifle of the Guatemalan Army during the years of internal conflict, the name became synonymous with rifle among the population.

words from the officer, having come so close to putting a bullet in her head.

They bring her things off the bus and she's taken to the detachment's quarters where she is reverentially treated with everyone running around trying to put together a reception worthy of her. The soldier was punished but Martina asked for it to be lifted as he was only doing his duty. She admits her fault since it was her nature to react without thinking of the consequences. In her presence, the punishment was lifted; however, knowing the unpredictable nature of military discipline, she never really knew what happened to him. She stays for a couple of hours and the officer pulls a car off the highway telling the driver he answers with his life if she doesn't reach her destination in one piece.

Julia registers Martina in the village's local school the following year. She doesn't want her risking her life every time she travels and Martina had no choice but to obey.

During her term as madrina she's had to attend many social events. The first time they come to pick her up, people assume she is in trouble and that's why the army came for her in a jeep, like all the other beauty queens. Rumors are settled after Julia almost rips the hair of a woman who dared slander her granddaughter.

The decision to leave for a new destination

has arrived. Martina turns eighteen and gathers the family to tell them of her decision.

Her grandparents cannot believe their ears. They have worked so hard, saved all they could to pay for her university and now she comes up with that! She only asks for a blessing from her angels for, without them, she won't make her dream come true. Julia scolds one of her nephews, a human trafficker, believing he enthused her to travel. Martina explains this is not the case. Julia places her savings, the ones destined for her university, on her nephew's hand as payment for the trip and expenses. He tells her not to worry, nothing will happen to her little girl as long as she's with him, he'll care for her like his own sister. Julia also places her trust on that man, who's sworn to her Martina will move in with one of his sisters, who lives in Los Angeles, California for the last couple of years.

The grandparents take Martina across the border and tell Juan they will meet them at the Tuxtla Gutierrez bus station to say goodbye to her. Julia's intention is to take her to meet her uncle and say goodbye at the same time, wanting to give them closure. Arturo is shocked when he sees Tomás, they hug each other tightly and shed many tears. Tomás meets his niece and she her cousins, everyone saying goodbye to Martina.

Julia is flooded in tears and Arturo cannot

stand the know choking his throat and holding his wife tightly tells her:

—Let's be strong, woman, our little girl's wings have grown and she wants to fly on to new horizons; all we can do is pray for her.

Disconsolate, they return home in each other's arms.

Martina is seated by the window, as she usually does, her eyes bloodshot from all the crying. Next to her travel two other young ladies with whom she starts talking and with a Mexican accent one of them asks:

—Where are you headed?

Martina says:

—I'm going to start at the university and will be staying with my grandma… I'm so sad having to leave the place where I've lived my whole life.

The young ladies agree with her feelings and the fictional place Martina invented; they tell her they're also headed to the same university. They haven't traveled far when they reach the first checkpoint. Many green-clad men climb aboard and randomly ask for Mexican identification documents.

Martina continues talking with the girls so as not to attract attention and one them mentions the streets of the place where they're going to live and Martina says:

—What a coincidence, my grandma lives

close to that street.

One of them replies:

—Let me write down the address so that we can be friends and you can visit us when we're settled in our places.

One of the immigration officers stops right by the row where Martina is, who felt like someone poured a bucket of icy water on her, when one of the girls says:

—This is going to be our address, not far from your grandma's house.

She extends her hand to take the note and smiles, raising her eyes straight into those of the officer, without blinking; he only gives her a military salute. Some passengers were detained and among them, two from her group. Martina sighs in relief and at the next stop everyone gets off the bus. The [64]coyote checks them into a hotel and asks Martina to take care of the fanny pack where they have the money for the trip, explaining he has to go back for those previously arrested, they are his responsibility since they're not too far from the border yet. If there is a raid on the hotel the manager will make a sign so that they hide. With those instructions the coyote returns for their fellow travelers that same night.

Martina is nervous over her responsibility for

---

[64] Coyote: colloquially a coyote is someone who smuggles immigrants into the United States across the US – Mexico border.

the money. She tells the other members of the group she has a bad feeling about it and instructs them to have their backpacks ready, in case they need to leave. They haven't touched the beds in order not to avoid suspicion.

Before ten at night they hear the signal; Martina leaves through the back and heads for the bushes. Behind her are the eight other members of the group, doing everything she does. She drops to the ground, just like she did in drills with the army reserve. She signals them to be quiet and not to move. The flashlights are visible in the distance, looking for something. They stay in the bush for a few hours until the hotel manager signals them to return. Once in her bed Martina thinks how her survival instinct drove her to that ravine. Not for a moment did she remember her phobia of vermin and snakes. She still remembers the bite that almost killed her when she was a little girl. Her guardians are not here now and she's alone and on her own.

A Colombian couple asks Martina to take them with her, their family already in the US will pay for the cost of the trip. They've mistaken her for a coyote and she explains that, just like them, she is just one more migrant. Juan, the true coyote, tells them they have a full complement though Martina insists in not leaving them abandoned to their own devices. Now they are part of their migrant caravan and Juan is none too happy, he thinks there are too many people in the group and they attract more attention this way.

At each stop they make at the places known to the coyote, they stay for two to three days until the road is cleared of checkpoints. In their group, there're two young Hondurans headed for New York; two more Honduran women, very different from one another, a sweet, fair-skinned lady and the other younger, bad tempered and black, headed for Los Angeles, like Martina. Two Salvadorans headed for Delaware; four Guatemalans going to Massachusetts and the Colombian couple, with Miami as their destination.

They've walked a long way and the coyote tells them it's not far to go yet and to hurry up or they will miss the freight train. Everyone sits by the road where they came. Far away they hear a train. They rise and start running but it's too late, they miss it. The coyote is furious over the lost day and almost yells at them:

—Whoever doesn't think they can make this trip, give up now. Don't make me waste my time!

—What will we do now?

Asks Martina with a contrite voice.

—Walk all night by the rail tracks until we find a roofed shack or something to spend the night, until the next train.

Is his angry reply.

Every shack they find is without a roof. It's imperative they find a roofed one because a storm announces its arrival. They're exhausted and sick of walking so much. The road seems endless when they finally find a roofed shack, under which they are relieved to just drop on the floor to rest. Just like the coyote warned them, each person should bring their own food, when hunger strikes... they'd want to eat the rocks of the road.

Martina walks around looking for something to gather water and finds an empty plastic container. When it rains, she washes it with detergent and sets it to gather water from a hole in the roof. She carries a small bag of detergent, first aid kit, toothpaste, deodorant and feminine needs just like her grandma taught her.

The next morning Martina goes to wash her face with rainwater. When she sees her empty container she feels consumed with fury. She screams and asks who dared take her water; they all look at the black girl. Martina has never been overcome by such rage and after taking a deep breath lunges at the woman, lifting her from the floor with her hands around her throat.

Juan separates them and tells her:

—Are you crazy?! You almost killed her... they'll make me pay for her as if she were German!

The woman doesn't even apologize. Martina

goes off to walk by the tracks to calm down and find some water to brush her teeth and freshen up. She finds a deep pool and carefully, as not to muddy the waters, she washes her face and teeth.

The emptiness and silence of the place is overwhelming, not a soul to be seen.

In the afternoon, expecting another downpour, they hear the train far away. They race to get ready and the train slows down, they have to climb it as it runs. Martina remembers her basketball runs and figures she will pretend like she's dunking the ball and starts running after the train. Already in mid-air she grabs the handle and gets on the train. Almost everyone is on board except for the black Honduran girl and the train starts gathering speed. Martina is worried about leaving her behind and, in desperation, climbs off the train, grabs her and with amazing strength lifts her and throws her onto the moving train so that the others can grab her. The train speeds up and Martina is falling behind, everyone screaming for her to hurry and finally she grabs the handle again and climbs onto the train.

Juan gives her an earful for her exploit and says:

—Many have left legs, arms and even their lives on this beast and everyone here is on their own, accepting the risk and whoever doesn't want it, can stay behind but I cannot allow anyone to risk themselves over another, especially you. Aunt will kill me if something happens to you!

He finishes by telling her:

—A few hours ago you almost killed her and now you help her? What's the deal?

Martina says:

—That was different, I only wanted to give her a lesson. We're all one team and we gotta help each other.

They continue on to Acapulco; the heat is stifling and they are suffocating, out of water and under the blazing sun. They arrive at noon and check into a motel to shower and change. It's time to take a chance in the bus to Mexico City. For this Martina wears a long sleeved green turtleneck, her favorite color, a short black skirt, three inches above her knees, black pantyhose and black shoes with a buckle on top.

Their challenge is not running into an immigration checkpoint even as Martina has no problem imitating the local accent, which she has practiced for over a year; the rest can't even open their mouths or they automatically give themselves away, the black Honduran woman is the one most at risk. After Martina saved her she apologized and now won't leave her side. Juan gives them money to buy their tickets separately. Martina asks Juan to allow them to travel in twos. Her partner is the dark skinned girl. Before leaving the motel Martina tells her to pretend to be a mute, not to say a word or make a sound no matter what. She shouldn't say anything and she will pretend they are cousins. Everyone looks at her, aghast, over the risk she is taking on.

She tells them:

—Anyone can have a black cousin, what's the big deal?

No one says a word, the contrast is clear. Everyone buys their tickets except for a member of their group who is illiterate; he asks Martina to repeat what the coyote said. She quietly goes to the window and asks the cashier to help the man purchase a ticket for Mexico City. That small indiscretion creates a huge problem since now the bus driver and his assistant figure out they are all undocumented migrants and assumes Martina is the coyote.

The assistant checks the tickets before departure and asks Martina to get off, there's a small problem with her ticket. Martina naively gets off the bus and he tells her to give him fifty [65] **pesos** per person or he is going to denounce the entire group to the immigration service. He tells her he knows they are Guatemalan and she will go to jail as a coyote. Martina is stunned and sees a patrol coming near. At the breaking point, she takes a deep breath, fixes him with a stare and

---

[65] Pesos: the national currency of Mexico

almost yells at him:

—Look, you son of a bitch! I am a Mexican citizen and no [66]güey is going to extort me. My cousin is mute and we're going to [67]*el de efe* to see her doctor but we'll see who's who here!

As she finishes these words she whistles loudly to attract the patrol's attention. They stop, as if searching for the source of the whistle. The man is now scared thinking he got the wrong person. Going for broke Martina ends with:

—Of course you got the wrong person, [68]pinche güey, the one who's going to jail is you, if you keep on being an asshole. Move it, [69]puto!

Pushing the assistant aside she boards the bus again. She's shaking inside and when she reaches her seat, in the front row by the window, her alleged cousin fakes some sign language asking her what happened, and she answers the same way. The driver looks at her over the rear view mirror and Martina fixes him with an unblinking, icy stare. She doesn't sleep through the long

---

[66] Güey: Güey, pronounced "whey," is Mexican slang for "dumbass" or "idiot," although it can also be used more as a slang term for "man" or "dude."
[67] El de efe: The DF, Mexican colloquialism for Mexico D.F. (Federal District)
[68] Pinche: In many Spanish dialects, pinche is a swear word variously meaning "goddamned," "shitty," or "fucking," among other senses. The term literally refers to a low-level or temporary worker,
[69] Puto: Mexican slang for gay/homosexual. Puta: whore

voyage, alert for anything untoward happening, frowning and looking intensely at the extortionists.

Just as planned back at the motel, the coyote gets off the bus with the Honduran woman first, with the next pair at the next stop and so on, until they are all off the bus.

The coyote finds them, one by one, in a minibus and they head for a house. They spend a week there and then retake their journey. Two Guatemalans and the Salvadorans are left behind in Mexico City when their money runs out. The rest are guaranteed the full trip since their relatives have already paid the coyote's sister.

Still dressed as tourists the next ride is by train to Guadalajara. Their instructions being: once you get to the station, find the exit and head for the restrooms to change clothes.

Martina is distracted for a moment and loses sight of the group. For a while she feels lost and she goes to an immigration officer who asks:

—May I help you?

She feels her heart skipping a beat but recovers and asks him:

—Where's the restroom?

He turns around and points her in the right direction, where she sees the group. She notices they pretend not to notice her, believing she has betrayed them.

As she leaves she feels someone following her; she turns and finds the blue eyes of a skinny, good looking and fair skinned young man, about five foot ten inches tall, well dressed. Martina pays him no attention and enters the restroom. She rushes so as not to anger the coyote. They head for a supermarket to buy food and water for the longest leg of the trip is still ahead of them. Dusk is beautiful and they head for the train tracks. They find an empty car and once again face danger on another beast. Juan tells them this will be their five-star room, where they'll spend a couple of days until they reach Sonora. Martina notices again the young man from outside the restrooms is roaming around their train car. She tells Juan and he tells her he must be looking for an empty car as well, all they can do is stand guard.

Martina has a bed feeling and asks for the time, someone says it will be ten o'clock at night. Not even five minutes after that they are surrounded by bandits. Their boss asks who their leader is.

Juan asks:

—What do you want?

The same man, who a few hours earlier crossed paths with Martina, says:

—I want that woman!

Pointing at her and telling them:

—I have money, drugs… How much do you want for her?

Martina almost faints when she hears these words and Juan tells him his sister is not for sale. Not satisfied, the man tells them that before the train leaves, he'll be back and one way or another, he wants that woman. Martina, furious, tells them to get off to find whatever they can to defend themselves and they go looking for rocks, sticks, pipes, anything they can turn into a weapon, this has turned serious. One of the Honduran men tells her they will only hurt her over his dead body. The entire trip they hadn't said a word to each other. Martina smiles and thanks him for his solidarity. Before midnight, the criminals return. Juan tells them his decision is the same, his sister is not for sale. He's so angry he yells:

—Putos here!

Pointing to his right.

Putas here!

Pointing to his left.

And you, here!

Pointing at Martina.

They fight almost to the rhythm of the beast moving along the rails; Martina pushed one of the thieves off Juan just before he almost plunged a screwdriver in his back. She's beside herself, on top of the guy, slamming his head against the floor of the railcar. The others have already run away but she still beats one of them. She seems possessed and everyone watches in amazement. She bodily lifts the man and throws him off the car at the same time as another train comes along and everyone screams:

—Dear God!

Martina can't stop shaking, they hand her a cup of water and looking at them, like nothing happened asks:

—Everyone ok?

Some have scrapes and scratches in their arms, others have cuts and bruises in the face and head. She takes out her first aid kit and while she normally is not one to play nurse, she is brave and helps them all.

The next morning the train stopped under a large bridge. Juan says it's to pick up water, it always stops there. Martina is standing by the side of the entrance to the railcar when she sees the gang leader again.

Her heart beating fast she tells them all:

—Let's get ready, here they come again!

They all stand firm behind her, looking like a warrior queen out of an action movie. The leader has a stick with a white rag as a peace flag and when he's in front of their railcar says:

—I didn't know you're [70]La Patrona, I'm just

---

[70] La Patrona: the boss lady, a term of respect.

looking for our guy. Don't torture him anymore!

Unsurprised she says:

—We don't have anyone here, he took off running like the coward he is, same as the rest of you.

He insists on checking the car, which Martina authorizes, to verify they don't have his [71] achichincle. He asks Martina if she killed him. Martina tells him to leave them alone because she's had it and he'll be sorry if he bothers them again. He places his hands together to his forehead and bows to Martina. Everyone else is stunned, jaws hanging, over this.

She says:

—What are you looking at? I didn't spend my weekends learning karate and in the army reserves so that any asshole can come take advantage of me.

They can't believe she's become for all practical purposes, their guardian and protector. They arrive in Sonora at the home of the next coyote. Juan's part ends at the Tijuana border and then this guy takes over. He also tells them they will be there for a week, there's too many checkpoints lately.

It's the month of June and the sun burns down into your bone's marrow, water seems to come out the faucet almost boiling, there's no

---

[71] Achichincle: low level helper

relief from the heat. Finally they retake their journey and take a bus to Tijuana. The drive through the desert gives Martina chills, who as usual is seated in the first row next to the window. Her eyes can see many cars of different colors at the bottom of the precipice and the wind howling against the rock formations seems to whisper a chilling moan. The clouds form different shapes against the sky. Most of the passengers are asleep, their faces covered as if to avoid seeing a ghost. Martina recalls a song she heard on her grandpa's old radio, about a white horse, which climbed step by step the same mountain pass they are going through, as if he was carrying everyone's doom on his back.

Suddenly a gust of wind hits the bus making it swerve and some passengers scream in fright as Martina closes her eyes and asks God for everyone's life. The scare makes her fall asleep until someone shakes her saying:

—We're here, let's go, let's get off this bus.

They check into a small hotel in the middle of the city. From her room window Martina sees the daily bustle of people, so different from her village. Now she can finally rest her body and mind, she's had some tough days and they still don't reach their destination.

Guadalupe, the new coyote, knocks on the door of the women's room. Martina opens it and he asks if she needs anything. She says:

—I'm fine but let me check with the others.

All the women want is to rest. He insists and asks her:

—Would you like to go check the city out?

She answers:

—Same as them, I really just want to rest but I thank you for your kindness.

The coyote has noticed Martina since they left Sonora and is trying to get on her good side. They leave the hotel in the wee hours of the morning, as cold as the Sonoran desert was hot. The chill cuts to the bone and their hands grow numb if they are not wearing gloves.

They're all sitting on the hill overlooking the city, waiting for the change of guard on the US side. Martina is shivering and goes near Guadalupe who says:

—Hope you don't get me wrong, I offer you my [72]zarape.

In that moment, she doesn't care what his intentions are, she gladly accepts. He tells her that when they start running, don't leave his side, whatever may happen.

The coyote says:

—It's time! Everybody up! Any questions about what I told you, tell me now, once we're in the desert, all is forbidden.

---

[72] **Zarape**: woolen or cotton poncho, a shawl.

Everyone agrees with having understood his directions. Martina grabs onto his belt and they start running until he raises his hand and they stop. So it goes, stop-and-go until the morning light finds them. They hide behind thorny bushes and lay down, exhausted. There's a few water jugs and cans of food. The constant passing of migrants has had an impact on this spot. The ground looks like just-waxed flooring, with names and messages scratched on it.

Guadalupe tells them they will spend all day there, and won't move until nightfall. They hear sirens and helicopters and he says:

—As long as we stay hidden in these bushes, we're all safe here.

Everyone's laying on the ground, trying to sleep and rest, the heat is stifling and numbs their minds, all they want is to take off running. They hear moaning matched by buzzards squawking, maybe hoping for a corpse or someone unable to complete the hazardous journey. The wind feels heavy, as if it's trying to uproot the tumbleweeds from the dry desert to betray the dreamers hiding beneath. They can feel the presence of those who disappeared and ended up as fodder for the desert animals, never to be seen again.

Martina wets her red bandanna and puts it on her head, trying to block off the heat and not even hear the sounds of the desert. Dusk begins by turning the skies orange and red and a slight cooling in the air. It's like a fight between day and night, each one showing the depth of its entrails.

It must be around ten at night and the cold is pronounced, now imposing itself on the earlier heat, which tortured the living around noon.

It's time to get back on the road. Martina grabs hold of Guadalupe's belt again and he reminds them it will be the same as the day before: run, stop, run stop, walk, and they do this all night long, until dawn.

They hear noise from cars. Martina let's go of the coyote and tells him they must stop, she needs to pee, he tells her to wait, not much longer to go but she insists. He reminds her to watch her step because it's pig farming country and there are pools of wastewater from the nearby ranches. Martina screams and the coyote asks if she is ok. She tells him she fell into a pile of manure. Everyone laughs and the coyote silences them, it could happen to any of them. Those piles and pools are actually a sign they have arrived at their next hiding spot.

He tells them:

—We're here! Wait right here until I come back.

They're in the middle of nowhere under another bush and gagging from the stink of the pig farms. Martina ties her bandanna around her nose, to cover up the stench that's stuck to all of them. She removes her sneakers and socks and puts on her skirt. Slowly takes off her jeans and with it she cleans her feet as best she can. Just like at the previous place, there are traces of previous migrants passing through. At dawn she washes her feet with the water from the jugs and dries herself with a small towel she has, she even puts on perfume and pantyhose and her dress shoes.

The coyote returns for them; one by one he hides them under the cars' seats. Martina waits to see where she's supposed to go in such a tight space. Guadalupe tells her she'll go in front, no one says anything. He warns her that, should they be questioned, he'll say she's his wife. At the next checkpoint, Martina pretends to be asleep and thinks to herself:

«*My God! So many sacrifices to end up in these gringos' hands. Dear Lord, please, don't let ask anything or search us*»
Then she only hears someone say:
"Next".
When she opens her eyes, they are under way. The car stops to take them out of their hiding places and travel in some comfort. Danger is over. To calm her nerves, Martina turns on the radio and listens to the final game in the Copa America. They take them to a motel in Los Angeles from where each person is sent to their families, some

by air and others to live in nearby cities. Martina, once again, has an ill foreboding, like a tickling in her heart, when something bad is about to happen and it's never failed her so far.

Juan doesn't take her to his sister's house and when Martina asks what time is she going, he only says "soon". One of the Honduran men tells him his father can pay for Martina but he replies there is no need. Martina is feeling mistrustful and with her backpack, she waits in the motel's hallway. Guadalupe asks her to come in but she ignores him. She wracks her brains wondering what to do, in case they abandon her there or worse yet, if he has "other intentions".

Guadalupe comes to tell her:

—I'm very sorry but your relative says they won't accept you at his sister's house, he thinks you and I are together because I helped you during the crossing; he's telling me to charge what I want but he is not about to give one cent for you.

Martina is livid with anger, so much she can't even scream; her cheeks are flooded in tears, her mind, stunned; she cannot think clearly. She recalls how Juan was paid for the whole trip with the money for her education and wonders:

«How can he be such a jerk?? How can this bastard keep all the money my old folks gave him? He will pay for this!»

Guadalupe tells her she could go with him

to his San Diego house. She looks at him with tearful eyes and says yes, but if he tries anything she will scream and doesn't care if she's caught and deported. He tells her he just wants to help her and she better come into the room; she doesn't care about being outside, feeling safer since she doesn't know what his intentions are. Martina feels her head is about to explode from thinking all the thoughts that torment her. What will she do in this immensely big city?

She then recalls that a woman from the army reserve gave her the name and number of her best friend, telling her to go see her once she was in the US. Martina browses through her notebook with the names, numbers and addresses of her friends and family. She asks the coyote to call this number. They call from a payphone and call but the answerer tells them she doesn't live there. Martina almost faints when she hears this. She insists on asking about the lady and the voice on the other end tells her to leave her own number and when the lady returns from work he will give her the message, she lives across the street. Martina indicates she's calling from a pay phone. And then doesn't move from the stairs until five in the evening. She calls again and the voice tells her they're going to get her. The lady picks up the phone and asks what's so urgent?

Almost crying, Martina tells her:

—Ma'am! You don't know me. Señora Silvia gave me your number in case I had any emergencies when I arrived here.

She relates the details of how she came to be talking to her but she really needs a place to stay for a few days and a four hundred dollars loan to pay off the coyote. She tells her to put Guadalupe on the phone and agrees to pay and have her for a few days. Martina thanks God for He has never abandoned her. On the way to the lady's house Martina looks at the street signs and city names, as she thinks to herself:

«Such a huge country, everything is huge here. Well, I made it and now I'll need to stay strong to remain here».

—What are you thinking?

Coyote asks her.

She tells him she is reminiscing all that she has been through to get to this point and what a miserable bastard her cousin was.

—That damned asshole lied to my grandma, she trusted him and paid for the whole trip, it wasn't free. They even paid in advance for a few months of rent and food until I found work… that's what I'm thinking about.

She sighs and starts crying; Guadalupe tells her that, thank God, the lady is going to help her even without knowing her. She tells him nothing is free and who knows how she is going to want to be paid for that favor, but for now, it's all she got. She warns him:

—Don't tell anything to Juan about where I am and if that son of a bitch asks for me, tell him I ran away.

She finds some relief at meeting the lady, who tells her she's very glad to have her in her home. Martina thanks her for the solidarity. Opportunity begins smiling on Martina and she thanks God every morning for his mercy, knowing it's new each day. She learned since she was a little girl and continues believing it, that life is a gift.

After the three month trip and a few pounds off her frame, Martina breathes in California's air. After only a couple of days she finds a job watching the kids of a couple who are both pediatricians.

It's early Monday morning and Bertha dropped her off at the house where she will be working, an African-American family. Martina feels out of place, she hasn't worked a day in her life, the lady of the house speaks no Spanish and shows her to her room.

Martina will work Monday through Friday and stay at their house. By signs and a few Spanish words, she's figured out what she will be doing. And her exploitation begins. The woman had told her she needed a girl to care for her children: a nine year old girl, a boy of six and a newborn, in particular, so that the lady can return to work. The older kids go to school. Martina asks for the other maid who will do the remaining chores and she's told it's only her. She takes a deep breath and organizes her day to keep the three story house clean and have enough time for the children. The older children have left for school and the lady will stay home that week to observe Martina's work. She starts cleaning and after four hours she's only halfway done and is dead tired. It's time for lunch and she prepares them something applying what she learned from her grandma and when the kids return she serves them this food.

They won't stop telling her:
«*So delicious*».
She half understands but the girl says:
—[73]Delicioso!
And Martina smiles at them.

The lady indicates the children will do homework and she should continue cleaning. Martina only nods in agreement, the house apparently hasn't been cleaned in years and poor Martina feels like her hands are peeling.

The master bedroom is a mess, she doesn't even know where to begin. Standing at the entrance she wonders:

---

[73] Delicioso: delicious.

—What kind of people are they?

And remembers her grandma telling her:

«*Mija, remember that even if one's poor you one should be as clean and ones' clothes ironed as much as possible; one's own house should be well swept and the bed made; being poor doesn't mean being dirty, poverty is in one's mind and heart*».

So she sighs and decides:

—I'll start with the bathroom.

And heads for the huge bathroom. Though it may seem hard to believe, Martina is surprised by everything she sees, having arrived at an unknown place; where she stands stunned, again, at the mess and almost gags at the sight of the bathtub as she thinks:

«*This tub is supposed to be white. My God! What... does their color run when they bathe? Que [74]shucos!*»

Eyes raised to Heaven she asks God to give her strength to come out of this. The bathroom is transformed and everything is neat and tidy. She cooks again for dinner and the children are happy. It's been an exhausting day and to Martina it felt endless... and it was only the first one.

It's time for bed and she stays awake for a while, trying to figure out a better strategy for the next day. She remembers her grandmother again,

---

[74] Shuco(s): dirty, of people or objects.

who always rose at the crack of dawn because she could accomplish more during the day, taking advantage of the early morning and because "the early bird gets the worm". With that memory in mind, she falls asleep.

It's Tuesday and she wakes up almost at dawn. She thinks she can clean the windows and the yard while everyone else sleeps. When she opens the patio door, she hears an annoying noise that almost bursts her ears. The couple comes down in a panic and finds her scared with her hands over her ears. The husband opens a small box on the wall next to the main entrance and enters a code to turn the alarm off. Dazed by these events the doctor asks:

—What are you doing up so early?

She explains that she got up early because there isn't nearly enough time to do it all. He asks his wife why they haven't hired another person, as agreed. She doesn't understand what they say, which turns somewhat acrimonious with gestures and loud words from the wife who returns to bed.

With his broken Spanish he tells her to go back to bed and that the time to get up is six rather than four in the morning.

Martina remains awake in her room and writes a few verses in her old notebook from Guatemala. Since she learned to do it, writing has been one of her passions and she only gets to do it when she is alone or desperate.

She makes a traditional Guatemalan breakfast which the kids are enjoying already when the doctor comes down.

He looks shocked as he yells:

—Nooooo!

And starts throwing food in the trash. They wonder why their father is doing this. The food is delicious! Martina is scared and doesn't understand why, either. She leans against the wall not knowing what she did wrong. The doctor explains to her, again in his few Spanish words, that he'll make his kids' breakfast. She nods in agreement. He has them on a very restricted breakfast diet. The children go off to school and before leaving, they kiss her goodbye. She looks at them and, smiling, gives them her blessing.

She cleans the whole kitchen before going up to the rooms and hears the baby crying endlessly; she wonders what's the matter with it but recalls the day before the lady told her not to even glance at him. Martina is baffled by the customs she's seeing and starts wishing for a return to her country. She finishes cleaning the rooms and the baby hasn't stopped crying. She goes to the master bedroom and sees the lady, desperate trying to calm the baby down. She goes into the bathroom and her eyes nearly pop out of her. She cannot believe the tub is filthy again, wonders what's the possible reason, how can this happen. As she cleans, she thinks:

«This is scum, but... why so dark, again, does their color truly run off? I don't get it; yesterday I left it like new and now the toilet is also marked».

The baby's whines make her get up from where she is and go pick him up. His mother left him in bed, not knowing how to calm him down. When she sees Martina pick him up, she screams:

—Don't touch my baby! No toque a mi baby!

She repeats a few times as Martina looks at her with her big eyes and shakes her head as if saying "you dummy".

Martina picks the baby and burps him, tapping his back gently a few times after which they hear a roaring burp. He was in pain due to the gases in his stomach and he fell asleep in Martina's lap. Instead of thanking her, the woman shoves her out of the room. Martina only thinks:

«Ungrateful hag! Supposedly a pediatrician and can't even burp her own son».

Grumbling to herself she continues with her tasks.

Wednesday it's the same routine. She feels like she's lost ten lbs. in two days only, more than she lost in her migrant journey and thinks she will soon get used to it or disappear, as skinny as she is. The baby is crying, and the lady is desperately calling Martina, apparently the baby needs to be burped again. Gladly, Martina does it and he falls asleep in her arms again. She finishes her chores around five in the evening and she goes to play with the kids. Dinner is at seven and by nine everyone should be in their room, except for Martina who stays to clean the mess after dinner.

Slowly the week nears end and Thursday is here. The woman tells her to clean all the closet mirrored doors. Martina signals she already did. Grabbing her by the arm she takes her to one of the rooms and points at a dirty mirror. Her son's tiny hands are printed on the mirror, one she had just cleaned. She can't believe her eyes and only shakes her head. Meanwhile, the pool cleaner arrives, and the lady finds him to translate to Martina:

—Lady says you need to clean the mirrors on the closet doors; she understands you did it already but she's shown you the marks and doesn't like that you blame her son, he doesn't do it on purpose.

Martina replies:

—That's not what I said but, no problem. I'll do it right now.

He tells her:

—Since I've been cleaning this pool, I've noticed their maids don't last, they pay them next to nothing and treat them like slaves.

She goes back to clean the mirrors although this time she can't help but be angry and a few tears roll down her cheeks and remembers Julia once again, who told her one day:

«You gotta study, mija, better opportunities will be available to you. Maybe you can get by with what you've learned but once you have a university diploma, you will find a much better teaching job. I'm so proud of you, my little piece of heaven».

The woman's screams take her out of her reverie. She plays deaf and continues cleaning. The woman comes and screams:

—Mariaaaa!

She still doesn't answer and the woman, furious, grabs her by the arm and calls her "Maria" again. Martina looks her in the eye and whipping her arm off her grasp tells her, tapping her own chest:

—Me no Maria! Me Martina... MARTINA... Maar... tiiii.... naaa! Get it? Martina! Ok.

The woman is stunned hearing Martina, for the times she's screamed at her she only stays quiet or nods. The woman reacts and tells her the baby is crying. Martina, as she climbs the stairs to go see the baby, thinks to herself:

«This black bitch thinks because she has money, she can humiliate people. Oh, no!

Hopefully tomorrow Doña Bertha will come for me and I can find another job soon, because I ain't coming back to this one, ungrateful hag!».

Entering the room, she forgets her irritation and picks the baby up. He falls asleep again and she thinks:

«Poor baby… what a mother you have!»

Each time the baby cries, there she goes to pick him up until he falls asleep on her lap.

Friday arrives and she can't hardly wait for Ms. Bertha to get her, she's anxious, thinking:

«Oh, dear God, please take me out of this slavery pigsty»

She's been exploited and discriminated against; when Bertha comes to pick her up, the woman of the house tells her she will pay her a bit more if she stays one more day. It's her daughter's birthday and she needs help. Bertha relates this to Martina, who says:

—Please, Doña Bertha! Don't leave me here even one more day!

Bertha explains this to the woman saying that, regretfully, she already agreed to another job tomorrow and she won't be able to stay.

The children are crying out for Martina, they don't want her to go as the woman tells them she'll be back on Monday.

Martina thinks to herself:

«Hell, no! I'm never coming back».

Stepping out of the house, she breathes in her freedom. One hundred and twenty-five dollars is her pay of which hundred goes straight to Bertha's pocket, as an installment on her debt and twenty-five to pay for food.

The next day Bertha tells Martina to join her at the hotel where she works, where they need staff and may be a job for her.

Martina fills out a sheet titled "Application" and they help her fill it out, as everything is in English. She asks her whether she wants to start right away to which Martina gives an enthusiastic "yes". She's assigned several rooms to clean, Bertha shows her once how to do it and that was enough for Martina to become one the best maids they ever had, cleaning and finishing on time. That Sunday after work, Bertha's brother comes to visit, and Martina hears him speaking very good English with Bertha's gringo husband. She comes to him and asks, please, if he can call the woman where she worked this past week and tell her she won't be coming back, to find someone else. He tells her to leave it like that, she will realize it when she doesn't show up for work. Martina explains her grandmother taught her to be grateful and although she wasn't treated well, they did give her a chance to work and thanks to that money she has been able to eat and make a payment on the debt with his sister. Annoyed, he does call the woman and tells her Martina is not going back to work. Almost hysterical, the woman screams at him asking why she won't go back and offers to pay her more money. He tells her Martina is moving to New York. She screams some more that Martina can't do this to her, the kids have grown close to her, the baby cries and only Martina knows how to calm him down. Bertha's brother tells her there's nothing he can do, he apologizes and hangs up. Martina is sad for the children, but their parents didn't value her effort and the love she freely gave them. That has no price!

From two working days at the hotel she now has found, Thursday to Sunday and has already paid off her debt to Bertha as well as food and rent. She's broke but debt-free for that was killing her. Also, she believed maybe Bertha was upset because of the money she owed due to actions and a certain attitude she noticed but didn't understand. One day after work, Martina cleans and prepares her food for the next day. She hasn't said anything about being exploited and when finished just goes to her room. When Bertha notices she's not busy, calls her and asks to clean the yard or the windows or bathrooms or something, anything as long as she is busy with something. Martina tells her she's done for the day, but Bertha doesn't stop until she finds her something to do. Martina ends exhausted up every day and cries in her room thinking:

«My God! I got out of the pan to fall into the embers. At least there I got paid, here I pay rent and food and on top of that I have to work more; I know I must be grateful, because that's what mamaíta Julia used to say, but I cannot let her take advantage of me».

Every night is the same, Martina ends up dead tired from all the work she is doing. On the days she doesn't work at the hotel, Bertha cleans houses and brings Martina with her to help but never pays her a dime.

Martina meets one of Bertha's friends who works with a Korean family and tells her a friend of her boss' needs a woman to care for her children, Monday through Thursday; Martina thanks her and explains she works in the hotel and cannot take the job although the lady insists she meet the mother to make sure.

Martina meets the lady in question and introduces herself as someone recommended for the job, but the Asian woman doesn't speak but a few words in Spanish and tells her she needs a mature woman not a young girl. Martina insists she try her for a week and if she doesn't like her work, that's it. The woman, of Chinese descent, accepts her offer.

During one of her shifts at the hotel, Martina

speaks with the manager and asks her to take away her Thursday shift even if it means she works a double shift on any of her other days. The manager agrees but cannot give her a double shift.

Martina starts working with the Asian family, the couple are also pediatricians and work outside the city, going away Monday and returning Thursday evening. The lady gives her instructions for the job and they both agree.

On Tuesday morning Martina wakes up early and prepares the kids' school lunches and takes the six-year-old boy to the school bus stop. The teenage girl waits at home to be picked up by a friend's mother, as Mrs. Whang indicated the night before.

She returns home and starts the cleaning routine, fixes her own lunch with the strange foods in the fridge. Mrs. Whang prepared and froze the meals for her kids, so they need only to thaw them until Martina learns to make them. She feeds their beautiful dog, which brings back memories of the German shepherd that was her own pet. The dog is chained since he is as big as Kaliman was. Little by little Martina gets close to him and pats him; like he knew her all along, he doesn't stop wagging his tail.

She tells him:

—My Kaliman! Have you reincarnated into this dog or what?

It's time to pick up the boy at the bus stop and he smiles when he sees her. They're walking back home when she hears her name and when she turns, wondering who would call her in a city where no one knows her, she hears tires screeching. A window is lowered, and she recognizes the African American family that exploited her. The woman only shakes her head angrily and tells her children not to mention Martina ever again. She doesn't believe the coincidence of being back working in the same area she did before. She walks on and talks to the boy, as if he could understand what she says, until they reach home. An hour later the young girl returns and goes straight into her room.

Martina serves the boy the meal his mother left for him, but he wants whatever Martina made for herself. His sister comes down to eat and her brother tells her to try it, it's delicious and she signals Martina to serve her some. When they finish eating the boy plays and watches TV for a bit, while Martina cleans the kitchen and the girl goes back to her room. It's time for homework and Martina tries to help the boy, even if only through signs and gesturing.

For dinner time, she thaws the food their mother left. She bathes the boy, puts on his pajamas and tucks him in bed. He's afraid to be alone in his room and hugs Martina, as if to ask her not to leave him alone and she takes him to her room, to sleep with her. That was their routine until Thursday when Mrs. Whang returned; she quite likes her house clean and tidy and her children well cared for. She's hired!

Those were the best days Martina had, being at peace, especially. Mrs. Whang tells Martina to take the boy to his friend who lives on the next block on Monday and Wednesday. That day she's happily walking with the boy and hears her name again. Walking by the house where she used to work, the woman is furious because she feels lied to when Martina refused to go back to work for her. She yells at her kids telling them not to speak to them, but their innocence and the love Martina gave them is stronger than any bigotry. Every time she walks by that house the children always say hello and there's no way to avoid it since it's the only street leading to the Korean family's house. Martina knows nothing of other cultures and realizes how different they are from one another. She feels more closely identified with the Asian culture, so much like her own with similar values and principles.

The steady work with the Whangs, the hotel and the house where she lives has revived her; she asks Bertha to borrow the telephone and she asks where she wants to call; Martina answers that she wants to talk with her grandmother. It's been many months since she last talked to them, only sending them money by mail but now she really needs to talk to them. Bertha asks for the number; Martina sees the dial turn and turn as she enters the digits. Finally, she says:

—It's ringing!

And hands the phone over to her. The long "beep, beep, beep" makes Martina nervous... Bertha returns and hangs up, ending the call and saying:

—If it rings too many times and no one answers, you get charged for the call.

Martina is surprised and says:

—Things are so weird here! In Guate if there's no answer, the pay phone would give my coin back and at Don Mario's store they didn't charge me, either, if there was no answer. It's just weird!

Bertha abruptly takes the phone from her hand and says dryly:

—Forget about Guatemala, you are in the United States now, you can try again tomorrow.

Martina thanks her and goes to her room. She writes about people's ignorance and the exploitation of new arrivals by fellow immigrants. Marco's words come to mind:

"When ignorance overpowers reason one must run from there".

And she thinks:

«And where am I going to go? I don't know anyone».

With Marco's and Julia's memories, she tries to rest on the carpet of that empty room.

After an exhausting week of work, Martina accepts an invitation to go window shopping. One of her co-workers has been inviting her. She showers and half heartedly fixes herself up, but Bertha tells her that she doesn't need to dress up for cleaning. Martina tells her again that she already did her cleaning work and she's going to the mall with Karina. The woman grabs her by the arms and yells that she isn't going anywhere without her permission. Martina reacts sharply and releases her arm from her arm. Very serious she tells her:

—Look, lady! I've put up with enough from you because you were kind enough to take me in but I'm not going to be your slave for life. I've more than repaid your favors.

Furious, Bertha tells her:

—If you leave now, never come back!

Martina starts packing as she tells her she'd rather live in the streets than be her maid, for free, without even a simple 'thank you'. Seeing how serious she is, Bertha changes her attitude and tells her she does love her like a daughter and that she's only looking out for her welfare; like nothing happened, she takes her arm and says she will join her.

Martina has no option but to accept. They arrive at the mall and Martina is distracted looking at the displays in a store. Standing like a mannequin she sees some dresses she'd like for her grandmother. After a few minutes she decided to go in and find out the price. When she turns, she runs into a gentleman who says:

—I'm sorry!

She answers:

—No problema, ok.

The man apologizes some more, and Martina is impressed and thinks:

«It's him. He's the man I came here for, the one I've seen in my dreams».

Martina can hardly believe her eyes, recalling the dreams she had of a man like the one before her. Her memories turn to a few years back, to the moment when she decided that the migrant destiny was the one for her. Despite the love and sacrifices of her grandparents so that she wouldn't lack for anything, nothing could convince her to stay in the place of her birth. She used to think not only how her grandparents were getting older but also how circumstances were growing more chaotic by the day in her native country... those were her thoughts when Bertha returns and asks what happened, Martina tells her. The young man apologizes to Bertha, thinking she is Martina's mother. He speaks a little Spanish and tells them:

—My name is Erick Meyer, nice to meet you!

—I am Martina Barrios.

Says she, holding his hand. Her brown eyes lose themselves in the greenish stare of such a handsome young man. He insists on buying them a cup of coffee and they cannot refuse his kindness and accept it.

He scribbles his name and number on a napkin and Martina tells him she doesn't have a telephone. Bertha makes her look like a liar when she writes her own home telephone number on another napkin and tells him this is her number. Martina completely forgot she was even going to buy a dress for her grandmother. She's impressed seeing the man of her dreams is real and he even has the same name as in her dreams. Her expression has changed. He says goodbye with a smile, promising to call, as she smiles back. There's no such thing as coincidence and it looks like the Universe is rewarding this generation with a new destiny.

Martina takes advantage of the trip to the mall and buys a few things she needs; some she likes and the dresses for Julia. When they return home, she asks Bertha to please make the call. This time, they pick on the first ring. She sighs with joy and asks to speak with her grandma. And they tell her to call again because they have to go find her at her home. They cry endlessly on both ends of the line, her grandmother thanks her for the money she's sent but is so sad over her recent decision. Martina doesn't understand and asks her to explain. Sobbing she tells her what Juan said to make her so sad: that Martina had gone to live together with the coyote, Guadalupe. She denies this falsehood and tells her that through God's mercy and the protection of their grandfathers and grandmothers, she is fine. Martina promises to call once a month, as expensive as calling is. Her grandmother tells her she understands. Martina's calls have been dearly paid, for Bertha shows her the invoice with the balance of long-distance calls but never her own. On the first invoice, she spent almost half a month's salary.

Love comes to brighten Martina's life with shades of fall and cool raindrops. She's been talking with Erick for months, never going on a date. After such insistence, she accepts the invitation of the man of her dreams. She's afraid of the fact that he's only a dream.

Many more came after their first date; she hardly even notices Bertha's upsets and warnings anymore. She's afraid her maid-for-free may leave the house; in one of their dates, Martina asks Erick:

—Why are telephone calls so expensive here

in the United States?

He's surprised and doesn't really understand what she means. She explains what Bertha tells her about her calls. He thinks maybe it's due to the fact they are long distance calls but promises to find out more on Monday and while he's at it, to get international long distance himself, for her convenience. Erick has become her best friend and the only person with whom she goes out, except for her friend Karina. They talk for hours, each about their own life. Erick tells her how he was orphaned when his parents died in an aviation accident. He tells her he had to suspend his architecture studies, auction off his parents' house and how he now lives in a mobile home. She offers condolences for his loss and the sadness of being an only child. They have both been surrounded by tragedy and they are both alone.

She makes her first call from Erick's house and when she hangs up after the third ring, he asks with surprise:

—What's the matter, why did you hang up?

She tells him once again about her experiences at Bertha's house and, laughingly, how she doesn't want to owe him a huge amount of money for her calls. He replies she shouldn't worry about how long she talks so she calls again and speaks for hours with her family. When the monthly bill arrives, she's sweating with anxiety about how much she will have to pay. She hardly talked on Bertha's phone and had to pay an arm and a leg! She cannot imagine how expensive it will be, recalling the long and frequent calls from Erick's house. She's stunned when she sees the bill, and cannot believe the cost of the calls. Bertha has charged her twenty times the amount, at least, can't even imagine how much she stole from her in total.

At the hotel they've asked her to work every day, but she cannot accept as she is quite happy working for the Whangs. She must decide and is pondering her options when Bertha tells her:

—The telephone is available to you to speak as long as you like, you haven't talked to your family in a long time.

And now emphasizes what a "bad daughter" she is. Martina patiently explains that she's been buying phone cards to better control her telephone time and spending. The woman wasn't expecting that and doesn't like the fact Martina won't be paying her entire bill now.

In one of their outings, Ericks asks Martina why she is so distracted. She tells him it's about work. She must decide and choose one of the two jobs but doesn't want to leave the Whangs. He tells her not to do so, something will come up to make up for it. That same day he decided to propose marriage to her. He tells her they are both alone and together they can accomplish great things. Martina has an answer ready; she's been waiting for his proposal since they met.

They start preparing a simple but tasteful wedding. Before the day of the wedding, Bertha gets some bad news from her family, one of her three sons died. She makes an emergency trip back to Guatemala; upon arrival she realizes she's lost precious time with her sons and now one of them is gone. After such tragedy, she renounces the materialistic life in the United States and tries to reconnect with her remaining sons; Martina never hears from her again.

They get married in the backyard of Karina's house with a few guests. The cold forces them to end up inside the house. After the wedding she moves in with Erick, after all, she doesn't have a lot to move.

Even after getting married Martina keeps working for the Whangs. It's Wednesday and she's about to go to bed but finds it weird the dog won't stop barking. The boy tells her it's because his sister's boyfriend is there. She jumps from bed and heads straight for the girls' room. Martina opens the door and they jump from the rug. The girl, screaming furiously, tells her to leave her room. Martina warns her she will leave but to get police, since she is under-age and the guy is there without permission. He takes off running, scared and the girl is very upset at Martina. That night, she cannot sleep at all, the tickling in her heart won't stop. After she's barely falling asleep, she feels a strong shake, jumps off the bed and hugs the boy. She hears the girl scream and stands still until the earthquake ends. Everything that was hanging on the walls is now on the floor. Mrs. Whang calls to check on them and Martina tells her they are fine.

The phone rings again immediately after she hanged and this time it's Erick, worried sick. She tells him:

—My love! I'm fine we're fine, God willing I'll see you tomorrow.

The boy clings to Martina, afraid, until the early light of day, without any sleep. School's closed that day. Martina cleans up around the house and picks up the broken glass. She makes breakfast and the girl doesn't eat, she's still mad at Martina for kicking her boyfriend out the night before.

Martina doesn't pick up after breakfast or lunch and waits for the doctors to return.

She tells them what happened with the girl and the boyfriend the night before and tells Mrs. Whang she cannot work for them anymore. Had she not made it on time, the man would have stolen the young girl's virginity. Mrs. Whang tells the girl to apologize to Martina and emphasizes that when she's not home herself, Martina has absolute authority and she must be respected. She tells her to follow her example, despite being alone in a strange new land, she married in white. Martina continues working for them after that incident.

On the days Martina doesn't work for the Whangs she starts a business, selling home care products and antiques in open air markets.

Martina suggests to Erick he should go back to college to finish his degree. He refuses, saying he has no time, due to work. Martina tells him she will take over their home expenses and will pay for his school, reminding him a year flies by very quickly, he hugs her and laughs at her offer.

Martina keeps at it and reminds him of her grandmother's words. She insists so much he does go back to college; after many sleepless nights, a lot of effort and sacrifice, Erick holds his diploma as an architect. Opportunity is wide open; he cannot believe he accomplished his goal and is grateful to Martina. He starts working at a construction company not too far from their home.

Martina had devastating loss with her first miscarriage. The sudden loss left her deeply depressed but rather soon when she goes for a regular checkup, the doctor congratulates her for her new pregnancy. She cannot believe God has replaced her loss so quickly. Erick wants her to stop working and rest as much as possible to avoid a repeat of the miscarriage. The doctor explains that it wasn't any physical exertion but rather, the baby had an enlarged heart and tachycardia so, basically, he had a heart attack in the womb.

Martina insists she must continue working while Erick is none too convinced and tells Mrs. Whang about his concerns. She tells him she will hire someone just for cleaning so that Martina doesn't perform any hard labor but please not to leave without Martina, who's been the only person to care for her children as if they were her own, despite her young age.

They reach an agreement and Martina continues working for the Whangs and tending to her antiques business.

MIGRANT DESTINY

SEVENTH GENERATION

In the last days of her pregnancy, Martina quit work. It's Monday morning and Erick has gone to work; he's just arrived in his office when he gets a call from Martina, her water has broken. He rushes back home and takes her to the hospital. They're both sweaty, either from stress or because it is a sunny morning, in the peak of summer. Martina is examined and her dilation is almost a ten but she's yet to feel any pain. They take her to the delivery room and one of the nurses whispers to the doctor that she's not feeling her contractions. She needs the baby out or it may suffocate on the way out. They inject her in order to force the contractions. Next thing she knows, she feels like she's dying from the worst pain of her life.

The contractions come harder and more often and the doctor tells her to push. So, she inhales and pushes with all her might until the baby is out.

They hear him cry.

She's drenched in sweat and Erick's been at her side without missing a second of the entire event. He catches it through the lens of a Canon FTB 35 mm video camera and so he saves the first moments of his son's life. He holds Martina's hands and together they cry with joy. Erick is emotional and kisses his beloved wife on the lips. They hand their baby over and they continue crying. Martina thanks God for the blessing of her beautiful son. He's taken into observation as he is jaundiced due to a genetic condition. Martina is discharged without her baby even as she tells the doctor she is not about to leave without him. He tells her that this condition could be fatal. She says, no problem, she will stay for observation, too. The doctor is unable to reason with her and gives her instructions for the baby's care at home.

Every other day, they go to the hospital to monitor the baby's condition. The doctor is surprised at how quickly he's improved and congratulates Martina. She can only think:

«*I've taken care of other people's children, how am I not going to care for my own?*»

The baby recovers fully and doesn't return to the hospital. Martina visits a pediatrician for vaccinations and routine care. Martina tells Erick to register the child as Erick Arturo; Erick for himself and Arturo for his great-grandfather.

Erick registers him as such, but with English names: Erick Arthur.

One month after the birth they go visit the Whangs. Martina brings her son to meet them and smiling tells her:

—I want you to meet the fruit of our love!

After the joy this causes Mrs. Whang, Martina tells her, with moist eyes, that she won't be working for them anymore and has come to say goodbye. She thanks them for treating her so well since they met, the trust and respect she was given and even the medication and attention she received during her pregnancy. They both cry and despite Mrs. Whang offering her a raise and to have the cleaning woman come every day, Martina asks for her understanding, as a mother. She says goodbye to the dog whose name she never knew and only called Kaliman. The animal senses what she is saying, and she cannot believe the dog is crying. It's been a sad farewell.

One week after Martina said goodbye to the Whangs, she gets a call from their house. They tell her Kaliman has died, Mrs. Whang tells her the veterinary doesn't understand why, it was a healthy dog. Martina cries for she knows he died of sadness, believing him to be her own Kaliman reincarnated in this new dog.

The baby is almost one year old, and Martina enjoys the life she dreamed of. To make her happiness complete, she gets the notice she's waited for many months. The next stage of her visa application is to return to Guatemala to get her "green card", as the residency permit for the United States is known. She prepares her trip although Erick won't be able to come with her due to an important project at the construction company. He's happy to see his wife travel back to her country after so many years. Once she returns, she feels her heart beating out of her chest. She doesn't really know what the situation is for, as far as she can recall, it's never known a period of peace and normality. When she left the country was still in the midst of an internal conflict. She doesn't keep up with news, has some reference about events from her grandparents and through a radio station she casually tuned into in her kitchen radio. She listens to the show every Sunday because they play marimba music and share some news about Guatemala. This is how she learned of the end of the civil war. After signing the armistice, there was another crime wave, basic foodstuff prices are beyond the reach of most people, there's a medication shortage and illiteracy is rampant.

 She feels an electric jolt when the flight attendant says the words: "Welcome to Guatemala City". She closes her eyes, sighs deeply and sheds a few tears. Her baby sleeps placidly.

Her family awaits among the crowd greeting the arriving travelers. Their meeting is deeply emotional, everyone cries to the rhythm of the marimba playing a welcome tune.

They go by taxi to the bus station and take one called "Southern Rapids", the same line that killed her Kaliman years ago. She sits in the front row as usual. Closes her eyes and breathes deeply the air caressing her cheeks as she thinks:

«*My country! I've seen beautiful cities and everything pretty...but you, beloved land of mine, are unique, there's no comparison to your beauty. I will return as many times as I can... I cannot be away from the place of my birth. Blessed land! This is why I don't understand... Why does poverty consume your people, if we're so rich in natural resources, why so much injustice, why such violence, why racism, if we all come from your womb. Why, Guatemala? My eyes don't lie to me, when I see such beauty!*»

Her thoughts go to verses she believed lost from her memory, her face is wet with tears, such is the nostalgia she felt. The country is still the same... or maybe a bit worse off, the same potholes in the highway; or maybe bigger and deeper. Without hope. The same structures or maybe they're more broken down, less greenery. The five-hour drive to her village she spends enjoying what little scenery is left, little by little mutilated by industry.

It's such a big joy for all to see her again, she left alone and returned with a treasure. The baby is blonde, and fair skinned like his father, with hazel eyes sometimes turning green and the Cabrera mole by the upper lip. The boy is about to turn one year old and the grandparents have put together a big party. A Christian service to present him before God. They have commissioned the most delicious cake ever baked in the village and a massive turkey [75]tamaleada made by Julia. They've gone all out, it's a huge celebration!

The young pastor Martina knew as a girl is long gone. The new one asks her if she attends any congregation in the United States. She answers that no, very little, but she seeks God each day. He starts preaching fanatically, which is the reason she fell away from church, they preach one thing and do another. She's very clear on the concept of God's love and says:

—With all due respect: everyone loves God and I mean this literally; we've been taught to worship and seek him out in many ways, different cultures, different languages and colors; but he is still all-powerful, all-knowing, the same of yesterday, today and ever; the alpha and the omega; his home is our heart and for this reason

---

[75] Tamaleada: the making of a huge amount of tamales (with turkey in this case) numbering in the hundreds, reserved for the most important celebrations.

we must keep it pure. The church is our body, it must be without sin; and the devotion of faith, his sanctuary; but we do the opposite, we forget to love our neighbor and no one teaches respect for life, to another human being, to nature... we talk so much about God yet we don't' lead by example.

The pastor didn't know what to say, he just congratulated her for her lovely baby and walked away.

Martina goes to the market with Violeta and upon their return, she hears a voice:

—So... this gringo-looking baby... whose is it?

Martina recognizes that voice and races to the door, she's burning with rage and almost yelling she says:

—It must be that coyote son of seventy thousand whores!

Juan is shocked to see Martina at the door and says:

—I was only joking with auntie.

Martina is flushed with fury and wants to let out the rage she's felt for many years and says:

—From this moment on, you're not welcome in my home and I never want to see you set foot here ever again. Never! Be grateful I don't curse your entire family but, you... YOU will kick the bucket soon, you bastard!

Julia shivers at Martina's words for she

knows her words have a power of justice and carry a sentence. From that day on, Juan never showed his face around their home.

Martina goes to the store looking for duvalines and cannot find any. They tell her Doña Tere might have some. She walks another block with her little son and finds the darn duvalines in that store. The lady tells her:

—You're Violeta's daughter, right?

Martina says 'yes', and the woman goes on:

—He's your kid, right?

Martina only nods, agreeing to what she says.

—Mmmm! He looks just like his grandfather!

Martina looks her in the eye and says:

—What do you mean, lady? You have no idea what you're saying, my son's father is not from around here.

The lady insists that she's not talking about his paternal grandfather but rather about her father. Martina grabs her things and with a stare from her brown eyes she thinks:

«[76]*Vieja shute!*»

The woman's words remind her once again of what she's almost forgotten over all these years.

She asks her mother once again and she receives the same answer as before. She says goodbye to everyone except her mother, she's mad

---

[76] (Vieja) shute: Nosy or in this case, "nosy hag"

at her because she has never wanted to tell her about her father.

She returns home and goes back to the sale of home products and her antique store.

During one of her trips to the community pool of their **mobile home park**, she's lost in thought:

«*I'm going to talk to Erick to tell him it's time to buy a house, our son is growing, and we cannot live all the time like sardines in* **a mobile home**»

During dinner she mentions it to Erick who tells her he already had thought about it, he's even designing it himself. She tells him that while they find the land and start building it, they should buy another home and sell it once the house of their dreams is finished. Erick isn't too convinced, but the boy is growing up and needs his own space.

Martina tells her husband that she will find them a home "con las tres B" and, of course, he has no idea what she means when she uses Guatemalan colloquialisms. This time he asks:

—Sweety… what's "the three Bs"?

She tells him with a smile:

—[77]Buena, bonita y barata!

He rolls his eyes, still not understanding her. Martina checks the home listings in the newspaper, nothing catches her eye. On

---

[77] Buena, bonita y barata: Good, pretty and cheap

Wednesday she anxiously awaits the "Penny Saver" magazine where she finds items for the antique store.

Her eyes light up when she finds one that grabs her attention. She calls the listed number immediately and makes an appointment to go check it out.

"Buena bonita y barata" she finds her new house in an exclusive residential area. Erick cannot believe that the monthly payment will be the same as he pays for his mobile home rental. The one happiest about it is their son, he loves being in the water and now has his own pool. They spend their first Christmas in their own home and their son is so happy now that he has his own room and space. Erick tells Martina he loves her more each day but especially that he respects and admires her. He couldn't have picked a better woman for his wife and mother of his child. She tells him that everything one sets one's mind to, must come true.

Life in the United States is nothing but routine; Martina realizes how different her quality of life is in each country and despite now having the life of her dreams, she has moments of sadness, missing her loved ones. Erick notices a sad look in her eyes over her family's absence and to stave off depression, suggests she visit them more often.

Martina visits Guatemala each year, without her husband, since his projects are larger now that he's an architect in high demand.

Erick hasn't been able to build the house he promised Martina due to his many responsibilities. She doesn't pressure him because their son is happy where they are, and she is also happy in the home they bought.

Martina enjoys multiple activities with her son and husband, when he joins them sometimes. She purchased annual passes to the most visited attraction in the world, one that all children dream of. Every chance they get, especially in the afternoons, she takes her son to the theme park. In one of those visits a Spanish speaking woman with a weird accent comes to ask her if she knows of any jobs around where she works, maybe she knows of one where they need a maid? She's newly arrived and needs a job. Martina tells her she doesn't work as a maid anymore. The woman apologizes, she believed the boy to be too blonde to be her son and assumed she worked for a gringo family. Martina tells her it's not the first time people think that. The woman mentions her sister brought her to the park to distract her a little, but she is desperate to find a job and that's why she asks every Latino looking person she sees.

Martina tells her it's a good strategy but most of the people here will be tourists, better to enjoy the day and God will put the right job in her way. Martina shares her phone number and asks her to call her sometime, maybe she can help her.

Upon their return home her son has a burning fever, Martina gives him medication to control it, but it doesn't work. Erick, frightened, takes him to the doctor and he gets antibiotics, but the fever persists. Going to the market, Martina buys some pepper, just like her grandmother did. On the grill in their patio, she lets the embers heat the peppers which she then passes all over her son's little body. When she burns the pepper grains, it looks like fireworks, after which the boy recovers as if nothing just happened. She thinks to herself:

«*That woman gave him the evil eye!*»

Erick watches in suspense and Martina hugs him and tells him those are her ancestors' beliefs and they happen to be effective. The woman never called her.

When the boy is three years old he starts attending kindergarten at a school near their house, he's very smart as Martina, since she had him in her womb, has instilled in him good customs and manners, educating him just like she was educated. She wants to make a good contribution to the world, leave a good seed and to conserve good manners.

She wants to pass on to this generation the values and principles, a heritage of art and culture from her ancestors. Just like Marco used to tell her.

A few problems arise at school. The teacher calls Erick's parents to tell them she doesn't understand what he says, his words are a mix of Spanish and English, so she suggests to them to only teach him English as it is the language spoken in his country. Martina is vexed and while she repeats the different words and the differences to him, he's so little he doesn't get it when his mother speaks to him in Spanish and his father in English.

Under the light of the moon they enjoy a lovely summer in their pool, when Erick tells Martina:

—Mommy, mommy… look at the moona!

Martina tells him:

—Beautiful moon, my angel, just like the beauty of your eyes and glowing like your innocent soul, son of mine.

Martina's eyes tear up because her son believes he's saying the words correctly. He created his own meaning, with a new word, when joining half of the English word "moon" and the Spanish "luna". So as not to confuse him anymore, Martina decides to stop teaching him Spanish.

She doesn't want her son to be discriminated against because he speaks a different language.

She remembers her own people being discriminated against for speaking their own mother tongue. Some allow it to be lost due to the marked classism, racism and discrimination in their countries of origin. She doesn't want to confuse her son, as she so often saw in her country. Many of the children of the original peoples don't speak their native language but neither do they speak Spanish, and this keeps them from being understood by their own parents. Big mistake, Martina's decision not to teach Spanish to her son, because she doesn't speak English very well and they become another statistic among immigrant parents who lose their own language with their children.

Somehow, with half-words Martina understands her son, through the love that joins them and though language is a great barrier in their communication.

After ten years Martina suffers the consequences of having accepted the teacher's suggestion about teaching him only one language.

She's decided to study English herself and improve communication with her son. Although his father helps him study, she also wants to be part of that.

She registers in the morning courses of an adult education center and her routine gets heavier. She drops her son off in school, rushes to be in time for class and then to the antique store.

She abandoned direct sales except for sales of skin care products since she is also a consumer of it due to its better pricing and has also become a consultant. Her allergies prevent her from using any cheap product and this company has amazing products that are beneficial to her. Even though she's only registered as a personal user, she has shared on occasion with people who ask her: "What do you use to have such healthy skin?".

The group director invites her to different conferences offered by the company. In one of those Martina had to present during the conference; her first words were:

—I have neither nor the money of a movie star, to spend life in a luxury spa. So, to keep my skin looking like theirs and spoil myself... I bring my own spa home, with quality products at a great price.

They all liked this message and from that day, the director invites to be part of the conferences and becomes one of her best friends.

The alarm bell rings every morning at the same time. Erick has become a little lazy getting out of bed and delays his mother with her other activities.

This morning, she dropped off the boy at school but returned home. She forgot her English homework. When she grabs the folder from the desk, she sees a blinking light in the message machine, which she finds weird because she deleted them all before leaving but she hits Play to see what it's about. She stands there, paralyzed for a few minutes, feeling her home crumble around her. Her husband had a serious accident and is in serious condition.

She goes back to school to get her son and together they head for the hospital. She tries to be like an oak to inspire strength in her son, although she feels like she's dying inside. When they arrive at the hospital she inquires about her husband and the doctor tells her he wants to see her. She asks if her son can come with her and the doctor allows it, knowing that Erick will not survive and needs to see his family one last time. They're in front of Erick, their son cannot help it and breaks out crying from seeing his father badly injured. Erick asks them to hear him out, without interruption. He asks them to forgive him for leaving them but also to remember they both have been his life and they made him the happiest man on the face of the planet; that choosing Martina as his wife and mother of his son was the best thing he could have done in his life.

He's been blessed with a wonderful son and an extraordinary woman. When he's done speaking, he asks his son to get close and places a kiss and a blessing on his forehead. Martina can't help herself and says:

—You swore you would never leave me; you cannot go, my love, you cannot go! Not now!

The knot in her throat keeps her from saying more and Erick asks her as well to come close. He gives her a passionate kiss, sheds tears that mix with her own.

—Te amo, mi bella Martina! Te amo, hijo mio! Los amo!

His last words are said in Spanish and, with a sigh, his life is gone.

The heart monitor flatlines and a medical team rushes in to revive Erick. With a broken voice, Martina tells them he is gone and not to damage his body even more. The doctor knows she speaks the truth and signals the nurses to stop the reanimation procedure.

Erick's death caught Martina by surprise, she did not have time to cry for him or to get depressed; she must remain strong for her son.

Making arrangements for the burial really took a toll on her. Sometimes, alone in her room she spills her sadness without her son knowing. She had started her English classes only a few weeks earlier and now she must drop out.

Her world has been overturned, she's full of pain inside. Mourning has withered the petals of her life and the only strength keeping her going is the great love she feels for her son. She makes sure to keep him well all the time and only thinks of giving him the best, just as they used to plan with her husband.

Erick has just turned sixteen and Martina feels once again the tickling in her heart that makes her anxious. Before the end of the day she gets the bad news, feeling like her world crumbles yet again. Her grandfather Arturo has died. Despite her aunt knowing he was her great love and she, the apple of his eye, didn't tell her when he first fell ill. The rest of the family didn't even know until it was too late. Martina doesn't leave her room for many days, she really falls apart, suffering for not having seen her beloved [78]viejito and give him a proper goodbye. When she comes to her senses, after crying her loss, she warns the family that if they don't tell her of anything that may happen with her grandma, she won't have mercy and will make them suffer.

She didn't communicate with her aunt or her mother, for different reasons, but the same intense pain.

Martina feels a pull, a need to travel to Guatemala and starts preparing her trip. Since she left her birthplace this will be the first Christmas she spends with her grandma. Erick cannot come with her; he is focused on his finals, but he wanted

---

[78] Viejito:Little old man; as mentioned before, a Guatemalan speech quirk is that making anything little, is a term of endearment.

to visit his mother's homeland. He only has vague recollections of it since he was very little the time he went with her.

Julia is seated in the old chair supervising the making of tamales which, traditionally, she always made herself. She would want to go make them again, scolding here and there about the right way to do something. Martina sheds a few tears seeing her faculties so diminished under the weight of the years. But her old spirit is still there. Her guardian angel is fading because of old age. Luisa asks:

—Why do you cry?

She tells her nothing's the matter, as she wipes her tears. Luisa tells Martina:

—Remember that nephew of grandma's, our cousin who took you to the United States?

Martina wants to know nothing about that man, but her sister continues:

—He was found in a ditch, shot, someone got even with him.

Martina doesn't say a word.

When Luisa sees her so quiet, she decides not to tell her about Doña Tere, whom one day told her about her father and died in a fire at her home.

She was already out of the burning house but remembered her savings were still inside and went back to get it. Her greed and lust for money cost her life.

After Christmas she says goodbye one more time. It's one of her saddest days, having to return. Being back in her homeland fills her with energy to continue the path of the migrant destiny she chose one day.

She's back home, back to her usual everyday routine.

Many years have passed, and routine becomes lifestyle. Martina is home one day, after an exhausting day at the store. Suddenly she feels that foreboding in her heart and tries to ignore it. Yet she continues thinking about it and before long, as she's lost in thought, she jumps, startled when the phone rings. The bad news comes from the other end.

Emergency trip. Her grandmother is ill and, again, Erick is in finals and cannot join her.

Martina arrives on time and goes straight to hug her special angel; breathing her last, the elderly woman says:

—You came! You're here! I thought I'd leave without seeing you, my precious child.

And extends her hand to tenderly caress her granddaughter's face. Martina, without ceasing to cry, hugs her closely and says:

—I'm here, madrecita!! I'm here!

The whole family cries disconsolately. The doctor's prognosis indicated she won't make it past tonight. Martina lies by her side and holds her like a baby. Sobbing, she thanks her for everything she did for her and asks her to forgive her if she ever caused her any pain. Flooded in tears Martina continues:

—I promise to keep your memory alive through your teachings. I love you, my darling viejita!

And she looks into her grandma's teary eyes. Julia squeezes her hand and gives her the final blessings, tells her she loves her with her whole heart and becomes agitated, struggling to breathe as her eyes slowly dim. In desperation, Martina starts screaming as she is surrounded by the entire family on Julia's deathbed. They say goodbye to Julia, at her ninety-five years of age.

It's a heartrending moment for all. Martina gathers her strength to prepare the wake, so very different to those in the United States.

During the wake Martina sees an elderly woman crying disconsolately at the feet of the casket and asks her sister Luisa:

—Who is that crying lady?

Luisa tells her it is her grandma's younger sister. Martina comes close to her and tells her she is Julia's granddaughter; the woman won't get up so Martina helps her rise from the floor. When she really sees Martina, the old woman jumps back, startled, when she sees Martina; she tells her in broken Spanish that her name is Chus and that she is Julia's younger sister. Martina takes her by the arm to sit her down and hands her a glass of water and tells her she never knew her grandma to have another sister. Chus tells her that due to some family problems they became distant and never saw her sister again until today. She tells her how surprising it is that she's identical to Julia's mother. Martina asks why she says that, she knows her family's history and she couldn't have known her, since she wasn't born yet. Maria de Jesús tells her she recognized her from a picture her father kept in his altar. La Chus confesses to Martina that when she first saw her, she felt herself shiver like she used to when she saw her father.

Julia is buried next to her ancestors and relatives; her gravestone inscribed: Julia Yoc Umul. The Meyer surname was lost when Demesio registered Julia with Martina's second last name.

After the burial, Martina feels dizzy. Goes to the doctor and he tells her, on the surface, she looks well but will do blood tests to make sure. The results come back, and Martina has chronic anemia and needs an immediate transfusion.

Martina doesn't want to be admitted so the doctor says, under her own responsibility, she must follow his indications. She hires a male nurse to do the recommended procedure. A few

hours after which she goes to the restroom. As she comes out, she asks for a chair as she feels herself falling; she faints as soon as she sits down but is still half-conscious, she hears the ruckus and feels a hand touching her neck and a scream:
—Noooooo!

Far away she sees a bright circle of light, slowly coming closer to her but also hears her mother's voice saying:
—Mother! Please don't take my daughter, take me instead but not her!

Martina is bewildered, wanting to tell her mother she can hear her but unable to get up at the same time; the light comes closer still to her. She hears the voices fade into the distance and suddenly the light goes out, blocked by a silhouette. Struggling to see who it is, all she can focus on is a woman dressed in white who is soon joined by others. Martina extends her hand to be taken, wanting to follow them but one of them shoves her back and she comes back to her senses. She finds herself surrounded by the whole family, all crying and asks what happened. In one voice, they tell her it's a miracle.

The grandfathers and grandmothers don't want her to join them yet; there's a long road ahead for her to complete and she goes back to her routine once again.

Time keeps marching on just as the sadness

she feels inside every single day, but her life goes on and so do her son's accomplishments. She's so proud he's the first one in her family to go to university. She marked a change in her generation, without knowing, becoming a born-again channel for victory ever since the previous generations lost their way.

He graduates with a history degree, with honors.

She continues working at her antique store and spends a little bit more time selling skin care products. Erick teaches in a university in Southern California and is undecided about two potential job offers he receives. He doesn't want to leave her alone, but she has drummed into his head that nothing or anyone should keep him from making his dreams come true. Erick has adventure and wanderlust in his blood and accepts a teaching position in South Korea. Martina is torn over his decision, however, supports him like her grandparents once did with her. Just like she took the decision to travel so far away and surely, her grandparents were as broken as she is now, they didn't say anything. In the same way, she gives her blessing to him for a prosperous life.

Erick follows his mother's footsteps, seeking a different MIGRANT DESTINY. Although his own country, the United States is a prized destination by others for its many opportunities, he takes a chance. Just like his great-great-great-great grandfather on his mother's side. Destiny rights itself again.

Erick works with teenagers at Seoul National University. In his spare time, he decides to get a master's at the same school.

There he meets Aysu, a young Turkish woman, tall and slender, with brown hair and hazel eyes, like Erick's, with silken porcelain skin, she doesn't even need makeup. Their hearts have bonded and have identical perspectives in life. Aysu comes from a family with values and principles of respect and love for one's neighbor, raised in a Christian home, just like Erick.

Martina is alone again and focuses her time on noble causes. She establishes a foundation to help support the education of needy children in her place of birth. She works with different Spanish-speaking communities, especially from Guatemala, to support their social labor.

Sometimes she also feels like she's had enough with some people's bad attitudes. Other women from her country speak ill behind her back without even knowing her. Some men, of dubious integrity, have slandered her. She knows who they are but doesn't use her powers to wipe them off the face of the planet; just by her getting angry they are doomed. She's lived in peace, with highs and lows, working things out on her own, until she got caught in the depths of some people's perversions. However, she refuses to activate the DNA in her blood and lets destiny take charge. She still shines with her own light and when meeting these people, she only smiles. It's her only defense to letting them affect her inner peace. This way, things settle down.

Martina receives an invitation to a gala event, looking more gorgeous than ever and followed by the envious looks of other women and men. She wears a lovely sleeveless purple dress and her hair down. Only for the second time she also wears the diamond earrings her husband gave her on their first wedding anniversary; she never stopped wearing her wedding ring. At her designated table there's a few other people and an empty seat next to her, where she placed her purse. Not before long she hears a voice:

—Excuse me, is this seat taken?

She moves her purse and looks in the direction of the voice and says:

—Oh, no. I'm very sorry.

They hold each other's gaze for a few seconds and the gentleman introduces himself:

—I'm Ernesto Gonzalez.

As he extends his hand to greet her.

She's deliciously confused before the handsome man:

—Pleased to meet you! Martina.

And shakes his hand, as he holds hers for beat longer and when realizing they're not alone, he greets the others:

—Nice to meet you.

Gesturing to the other guests. Martina has never danced in her life and Ernesto is an inveterate dancer. They exchange phone numbers and start communicating after the immediate connection they felt when they exchanged glances.

In her room she thinks about that elegant, skinny and tall man, with a unique skin shade, neither fair nor dark. He sports a few silver hairs on his head and grooves on his face, with wisdom earned through his year. She interrupts her reverie when her hand touches her wedding band. She believes Erick is sending her a signal and brings flowers to the cemetery, asking for permission to rebuild her life. Since Ericks' death she never believed she'd fall in love again. The wind blows softly revealing the answer she came for. In front of Erick's portrait Martina lights a white candle and thanks him for the love and happiness he gave her.

The Cybernetic Age is all the rage and most people seek refuge in social networking. Martina has no real desire to use them but due to her work, she's forced to open a few. She can see how most people's hatred is revealed through those pages and postings. She is tempted to play the game sometimes, but she remembers Marco's words, when he taught her to always try to be a better human being:

"Martina, you cannot argue with someone who doesn't have the same educational level as ours; that's how they were raised and you must try to understand this and just keep away, you could get hurt; there's people without scruples and they enjoy hurting others; someone else at their level will eventually teach them a lesson".

She sighs every time she remembers Marco and says that wherever he may be, he should know his teachings were not in vain. So, she ignores the social networks and focuses on what really matters. She's made some great friendships with people from many nationalities due to her business and social work.

Due to her son's absence and her own loneliness she's started writing poetry and even to paint. She's steeped in art and lets her creativity run wild, creating beautiful oil paintings.

She starts going out and is deeply smitten with Ernesto. Each date has a special detail for her, which is a weakness of hers and something in Ernesto's favor. He actively courts her daily and their thoughts are full of each other. During one of their encounters he asks her:

—Where have you been all these years?

To which she replies, smiling:

—My destiny was written… because my wish was to stay in Los Angeles and perhaps, we might have found each other then or maybe never. Nothing is ever late when it's the right time and nothing is too early when you have dreamed about it. We're together in our own right time.

Their arms embrace them in romance, falling deeper in love each day and saying it to each other as well.

Ernesto became a widower when his son was two years old and since then was both father and mother to Pablo. In their dates they talk of their country, its customs and culture, bound by the same ideals. Through Ernesto she learns about the Mayan culture and feels deeply connected with the teachings of their spiritual guides. She tells them she feels like she's already lived those same experiences.

The Tatas recommend she find out more about her roots, to understand this connection at the deepest level of her being.

They explain how God has given nature all the elements it requires to feed us, heal us and protect us. It's the elemental mother of our birthplace, that gives us life, feeds us and cares for us. They give her examples: how fruits and vegetables nurture us and make us strong; herbs are for healing us; seeds protect us. Everything has its reason for being and it has nothing to do with witchcraft, as fanatics allege. They continue saying:

—Evil exists and is real, there's dark souls which were born only to be instruments of destruction and we must arm and protect ourselves with the weapons [79]Ajaw gave us, which are nature and knowledge. The universe is infinite and God its creator. If we don't understand earthly life or human life, how can we expect to understand others' existences? We must care for what we have.

When they finish their talk, they light candles to light the way of this couple.

Martina meets Ernesto's son, a dark-skinned young man, with eyes black as night, impressively like his dead mother. A mental health professional, he works at a prestigious hospital and dedicates his spare time to music, his passion. He's connected amazingly well with Martina and through their mutual empathy have become great friends.

Ernesto and Martina decide to get married. This news surprises Erick but he comes anyway to be with his mother on her wedding day. It's a simple, tasteful ceremony with Martina's own touch for all special times in her life. Seems like

---

[79]Ajaw: Lord, creator, maker of the universe

everything coincides to keep on building alliances for the improvement of mankind.

They decide to rent her house and live in Ernesto's own.

He's surprised at her cooking skills, especially the fact she knows how to make tortillas. She tells him perhaps it's in her genes and laughs out loud, as usual. She tells him, step-by-step, how her grandmother taught her. Everything she knows and all she is, she owes to the guardian angels that were her grandparents. After many years, Ernest can finally savor authentic Guatemalan cuisine.

Erick tells his mother of his intention to marry Aysu and that they may probably live in either South Korea or Turkey. She tells him that wherever he plants his seed and is happy, she is happy as well. Erick asks her to write the recipe of his favorite dish, which he wants to share with his South Korean friends. Martina writes down the traditional recipe for shrimp ceviche and which is beloved by her son. She gives it to him with her blessings for when he returns to South Korea. He says goodbye to his mother telling her he will now be at ease knowing she is not alone. He leaves precise instructions for Ernesto and Pablo, leaving in their hands his most precious treasure.

Martina cares for Pablo as if he were her

own son; he's always lived with his father and hopes to find a good woman someday to make his own family. Therefore, Martina tells him to search carefully, for good women are in short supply and they both laugh. For the first time in his life Pablo has a mother figure at home and he thoroughly enjoys her until God places the right woman in his path. They have enough trust to discuss deep issues, as if they were life-long friends, just as she did with Erick, Through recent times there have been protests in the streets and in one of the conversations between Pablo and Martina, he asks for her opinion about them. She answers:

—We all have a right to protest but you must know what you are protesting; let me give you an example: if I tell you to put things in their place and I believe you understood because you are an adult who does the right thing and uses common sense. But, if you do not and ignore the rules, what could happen? Obviously, I would be angry and rather than argue or repeat things time and again as if you were a child, I'll just do it myself and put things back and we can go on like that for a lifetime. But if it bothers me, I have the right to protest and prove my point. So, for a protest, there must be a reason. In other circumstances people protest for change and it's acceptable. There have been changes throughout history due to protests although, personally, I believe change is achieved with a university diploma in hand, proving our generation can turn the wheel... but sometimes young people and some immature adults protest by destroying private property, committing crimes and to that, I cannot agree. Then they call you a delinquent and why would you want a criminal record and more, in this country? This nation, mijo, is diverse in social norms, with many influences from different cultures, we lose our own and take on another foreign one not belonging to us. We must keep our identity and respect others.

    Pablo listens intently to Martina. Time flies when they talk and there's always more to say. The same thing happens to Ernesto, long conversations that they can never finish. Speaking of migrants' issues Martina stares into space and Ernesto asks what's the matter; she says she would like to find her father someday and that would make her life complete. She believes that is the missing link she needs in order to close the cycle of bad luck. Ernesto tells her it's not bad luck, it may be bad decisions or circumstances beyond her control and promises to find him, together. Without her knowledge, he's been so close and yet so far.

    As a couple they are fully involved in migrant's needs and social work, which they used to perform individually and now they do as a team. It pains Martina to be defamed by unknown people who want to destroy their image. But Ernesto wisely tells her not to pay attention to such talk and to remain focused on their daily fight for the welfare of their fellow migrants. Martina agrees with her husband and says:

—Your words are wise and that's why I love and admire you; time will put each person in their place and all we can do is to keep on working to leave a solid legacy from our generation.

But her mind meanders as she hopes to figure out a way to stop people's evil from being passed to the next generations so that the world can find a better balance. She thinks:

«*Why do people like to defame others? Like my viejita, may she rest in peace, used to say: both are sinners, who kills a cow and the one who holds the cow to be killed; the one who defames others as much as the one who shares that defamation, I don't understand why they don't first find out whether it's true. Let God have mercy on those miserable lives and protect us from those people*».

Her thoughts weave into each other until she comes to realize that it's not only about prayers, light candles or burning incense, from a few; it's a matter of creating a new shared conscience for all. She thinks:

«*I feel in my heart that the makers of the*

universe have created a defense for a planet that hasn't awakened yet; by the heart of heaven and the heart of earth, I pray it never awakes or we'll be doomed to exile».

Martina has again connected her life to love and radiates an enviable joy.

Hand in hand with her husband they build alliances for young people to find their way and the old guard uses their knowledge to build a good future for the new generations.

Any generation's descendants spread through the world and we don't know who possesses a drop of the same blood... with stories to tell.

Starting today, a new history is written for a new generation, spread through different fates and genes born again.

New stories are woven, mixed from different heritages... forging their own way to a **MIGRANT DESTINY.**

The End.

MIGRANT DESTINY

REVIEWS

I've been delighted with Marla Rodas' Spanish language narrative; poet and writer of a universal dimension, pride of Malacatan, San-Marquean and Guatemalan who paints a magnificent linguistic work using "guatemaltequismos", the peculiar manner of expression of those born in this prodigious Central American nation, a reflection of a character's diverse states in life's stage. MIGRANT DESTINY presents a human being's generational landscape in key of seven, specifically within our geographic environment, with nuances where we see discrimination, evil, boldness, passion and despair but also how goodness, love and attachment to human values can overcome them and prevail in the end.

MIGRANT DESTINY is an interesting novel which must be inevitably known to the reader as a prized enrichment to our cultural heritage.

In this valuable and substantial contribution Marla Rodas teaches us a moral lesson: "Wherever you may go, show that you have dignity, your human worth, the traditions and customs are an essential part of the cultural mosaic of the universe and leave an indelible mark".

Congratulations, Marla! For this unequivocal delivery to our literature and my deepest gratitude for the privilege of expressing these words.

—**Respectfully, Carlos Roberto Munguia Sosa Teacher and writer, from Malacatan, S.M, Guatemala.**

My first experience reading Marla Rodas was of her poetry. I had no idea she delved into a novel until she presented her book this past summer. As a passionate reader I jumped into it the moment I got home and was quickly absorbed by the intergenerational story of the Meyers, Cabreras and the strong, suffering women that take center stage and propel the narrative from the late 19 th century to the present day.

During these past months I also had the honor of getting to know Marla better as a person and friend and it was a particular privilege to discover how much she has in common with her heroines of her tale. I had no preconceived notions or expectations about MIGRANT DESTINY and as an immigrant myself, it really took me back to that mystical side of my heritage as told by my grandmother since I was a baby. Yes, grandparents and grandmothers in particular are a vital, timeless presence within MIGRANT DESTINY and for every Guatemalan that remembers them as perhaps the single most perfect embodiment of love. It's no easy feat to take one back not just to a place or moment in time but a moment in our hearts and Marla managed to do this with this, her first fiction work, showing great potential and the promise of bigger things to come.

As an engineer by trade, something I wasn't prepared for was the "magical realism" in the story yet this is something we all grew up with, and as I remembered in Guatemala, I was also reminded of the growth that also drove me to eventually leave my native country and come seeking better prospects to the country my father admired so much. Her heroines' transitions from childhood into youth and adult responsibilities at a young age without losing their moral compass, the same one my own grandmother imbued in me and that kept me going, even in the darkest of times, resonated even as we follow their journeys into modern times, when there's no more shamans but

the fears and evils of political unrest are a far more present danger. Having also lived through that brutal period and having first-hand knowledge of the conditions that gave rise to that long and cruel war, the harsh discipline and military responses to any dissent, perceived or real, can bring chills to those who lived it and to those who did not, serve as a warning that freedom is human right, especially the right to travel freely across borders. No human being is illegal and in MIGRANT DESTINY we find just how much we have in common, whether we come from the same country or culture and how many of us end up making the same fateful decision that now finds us here as immigrants.

We are left wanting to know more about these characters and I would like to think this is not the last we read from Marla about them. There's yet plenty of material to be mined in those seven generations to really get to know them, their place and their times and how they came to be, think, believe and act the way they did here.

Here's to wish Marla Rodas a brilliant future in the genre and my congratulations and gratitude for letting us join her in this trip back in time to the simpler times we grew up in while also letting us see they may not always have been better. What more can one ask of a great novel? A true dose of magical realism and a portent of greater works to come.

—Jose Byron Gonzalez, Arcadia, California. January 2021.

MIGRANT DESTINY 351

ISBN: 978-1-953207-03-6 (5th book) Novel

ISBN: 978-1-953207-08-1 (4th book) Poetry

ISBN: 978-1-5323-4713-9 (3rd book) Poetry

ISBN:978-9929-711-00-6 (2nd book) Poetry

ISBN: 978-1-6176-4357-6 (1st book) Poetry

www.ingramcontent.com/pod-product-compliance
Lightning Source LLC
Chambersburg PA
CBHW031427160426
43195CB00010BB/636